FITNESS AND
THE URBAN WALKER

FITNESS
AND THE
URBAN WALKER

An easy-to-follow guide for people who wish to get fit, lose flab, relieve stress and energise themselves physically and mentally in a most enjoyable way

ERIC TAYLOR

BLANDFORD

First published in the UK 1989 by **Blandford Press**. An imprint of Cassell,
Artillery House, Artillery Row, London SW1P 1RT

Distributed in the United States by
Sterling Publishing Co., Inc.,
2 Park Avenue, New York, NY 10016

Distributed in Australia by
Capricorn Link (Australia) Pty Ltd,
PO Box 665, Lane Cove, NSW 2066

British Library Cataloguing in Publication Data

Taylor, Eric, *1927 –*
    The urban walker.
    1. Physical fitness. Walking – Manuals
    I. Title
    613.7'1

    ISBN 0–7137–2034–4

Typeset by Inforum Limited, Portsmouth

Printed and bound in Great Britain by
Anchor Press Ltd, Tiptree, Essex

Contents

Trad Not Fad!

Today we appear to be readier than ever before to face the fact that our health and well-being are largely in our own hands. It is helpful to remember, however, that by taking that responsibility seriously, we are not simply responding to a growing body of medical opinion nor, as some might say, to the whimsical notions of a few cranks. Some two millennia ago, Cicero had some eminently wise words to say on this subject, words that current medical opinion (including the holistic school) would echo.

> It is our duty to resist old age; to compensate for its defects by watchful care; to fight against it as we would fight against disease; to adopt a regimen of health; to practise moderate exercise; and to take just enough food and drink to restore our strength and not to overburden it. Nor, indeed, are we to give our attention solely to the body; much greater care is due to the mind and soul; for they too, like lamps, grow dim with time, unless we keep them supplied with oil.

Cicero in *De Senectute*, 45 BC

Paving Your Way to Fitness

'Not running, not jogging, but walking is your most efficient exercise and the only one you can safely follow all the years of your life.'

Quarterly report from *Executive Health Organisation*, California

A fitter, healthier and happier future is yours for the taking; all these benefits are free. But now is the time for you to pause, consider your situation and carefully make decisions. For this is no dress rehearsal; this is your life. The choice of how to live it is yours.

We all know now the risks we are taking when years of sitting at an office desk, behind the wheel of a car or in crowded commuter transport are followed by evenings slumped in a chair watching television. We are all well aware that if no regular exercise is taken to offset the effects of this familiar modern routine, the body soon reflects the inactivity. Sedentary living leads to ill-health. We look jaded and unfit; We age prematurely.

But in this ageing process there are more serious consequences than the loss of our looks to consider. They are death and disability. Diseases of the circulatory system — mainly of the heart and lungs — are the major causes in Western Europe, striking down people in their prime. Each year more than 1,000,000 Americans suffer heart attacks. But the situation there is improving, for when the number of deaths from heart disease reached epidemic proportions a new and alarmed awareness of the need to exercise caused people to change their way of life. They turned to various forms of exercise and then returned to the traditional one: *walking*.

Belatedly Britain and countries in Western Europe — still heading the league table of deaths from heart disease — are changing their ways too. People are taking more exercise, and like the Americans are turning to walking. For now they also know that the vigorous exercise from walking can have a protective effect upon the heart. It can certainly help us all to feel and look better.

Walking works very easily into the daily routine and as such a high proportion of the world's population lives in cities and towns it is the *urban walkers* who are most in the news today. They are using walking in a wide variety of ways to improve their well-being and enrich their lives.

Millions of city commuters have tried, at one time or another, various forms of exercise programmes. And they have found difficulty in keeping to a regular routine. When exercise programmes are not sustained, the gains made in one week can be lost in the following week of inactivity. Pressures of various kinds inevitably cause priority to be lost from taking exercise. Consequently, good intentions have foundered upon the rocks of family, social and professional commitments.

New Hope

Now, like a modern star of Bethlehem, walking brings new hope. It comes especially to all those who have, in the past, made sporadic and unsuccessful attempts at regular fitness-training. The 'good news' is that research carried out in medical schools and universities throughout the world points towards this one, infallible, simple, safe and effective way of becoming fit and staying fit – *exercise walking*.

Indeed, it is the exercise most recommended by cardiologists for patients recovering from heart attacks. 'It helps a person take control of the recovery process,' says Dr James Rippe, Chairman of the Centre for Health, Fitness and Human Performance at the University of Massachusetts.

But let us not fall into the trap of greeting walking like some new fad. There is nothing fanatical about walkers. Indeed, there is nothing really new about its beneficial effects on physical well-being. Throughout recorded history doctors have said that walking is the best, safest and most effective form of exercise for us all.

Twenty-five centuries ago, Hippocrates, often called the

father of modern medicine, told his students that 'walking is the best medicine'. 'But that was all so long ago,' the cynics might argue. 'What do the twentieth century "Hippocrates" say about walking as an effective exercise?' We could turn for authoritative evaluation to the US President's Council of Fitness and Sport. Their specialists say:

> Walking is easily the most popular form of exercise. It keeps the body energised and promotes physical fitness. Walking burns approximately the same amount of calories per mile as does running, a fact particularly appealing to those who find it difficult to sustain the jarring effect of long-distance jogging. Brisk walking of 1 mile in 15 minutes burns just about the same number of calories as jogging an equal distance in 8½ minutes.

In Britain the Health Education Council has this to say on the value of walking as a fitness exercise: 'The dynamic exercise from walking is an excellent stamina-building activity'. And the authority with perhaps the greatest financial interest in keeping people fit, BUPA (British United Provident Association), the non-profit-making health insurance company, puts walking amongst the highest rated of all health-promoting leisure time pursuits.

Why, one might ask, are men and women turning their backs resolutely against the more violent forms of exercise and the martinet instructors calling out: 'One, two; down and up; put some guts into it; this exercise is no use unless it hurts! Now! down and up; one and two'?

Chic dancing and aerobics studios from London to Los Angeles are shutting up shop and the best-selling books and videos associated with the 'sweating blood' cult of exercising are cluttering publishers' shelves.

Let us look at some of the evidence.

What's Wrong With Jogging?

On the morning of 19 July 1984 thousands of health-conscious people all over the world received a nasty jolt as they opened their copy of *The Times* and read about the death of a man who had made a million dollars preaching his gospel of health and fitness. He was known as the 'High Priest of Jogging' — Jim Fixx.

The report of his death told how Jim's best-selling book, 'The Complete Book on Running', had helped to push millions of people into the jogging craze. With Rambo-style sweatbands on their foreheads, absorbent towelling wrist cuffs and designer jogging outfits they had pounded the urban pavements and streets. These converts to jogging were shocked to hear that the author of that book had died of a heart attack while jogging in Vermont. He was a mere 52 years of age.

The mud-stained body of Jim Fixx was discovered lying across a grassy verge beside a country road, little more than thirty yards from the motel where he had checked in only an hour earlier. He was dressed for jogging in shorts and vest and had clearly dropped dead before really exerting himself.

Jim Fixx was known world wide for the success of his book — it had been translated into 12 foreign languages — as the jogging craze swept across the five continents. Within six years, jogging had made portly Jim, a one-time magazine editor, who boasted about smoking forty cigarettes a day, into a dollar millionaire. He was in great demand as a lecturer, preaching the gospel of jogging to fellow enthusiasts and telling them it did not matter what they ate — hamburgers, cheeseburgers, or pork sausages — for jogging would take care of it and protect the body from degenerative changes. He was proved tragically wrong. Jim might well have been fit to run, but he was not healthy. His arteries were clogged.

Medical Comment

Barely had the shock waves caused by the death of Jim Fixx subsided when six weeks later the jogging fraternity was shocked again, this time by a medical report which commented in a forthright manner on how the High Priest of Jogging had died and why.

'He ran himself to death because he had become addicted to the exercise,' said medical specialists. Ever since the age of 35 when he was very much overweight and a heavy smoker, he had run at least 10 miles every day. Running became an obsession with him! 'He was one of a group of hard-core running addicts,' said Dr Edward Colt, former director of the New York City Marathon Organisation. It was this addiction that killed him. Dr Colt then added a graphic warning: 'It could happen to anybody who is immoderately committed to jogging.'

So convinced was Dr Colt of this that he warned viewers of a British television programme called Where There's Life, which was shown on 24 September 1984, of the risks involved in over-exercising. 'There is a small group of people,' he said, 'who never learn. They are the hard-core addicts, brutal taskmasters to themselves.'

These addicts soon came in for further faith-shattering barrages fired by medical and sports specialists who deplored the over-zealous attitude to fitness demonstrated by many joggers. Dr Henry Soames, a cardiologist who wrote 'The Exercise Myth', said that 'if this exercise were a drug which had to be licensed, it would not receive government approval'. He back up this surprising statement with further shocking statistics about jogging. 'The death rate during jogging is seven times higher than coronary deaths during less strenuous pursuits.'

The message he then gave to joggers was spelt out in no uncertain terms: 'The risks are too high: death, hormone imbalances for women, and orthopaedic injuries.'

Most of these 'orthopaedic injuries', say the physiotherapists who treat them, are the result of over-exertion. Joggers would perhaps be well-advised to consider the words of United States baseball player Ritchie Allen who once said, 'Your body is just like a bar of soap. It gradually wears down with repeated use.' Somewhere between that maxim and the German one of *'Was rastet rostet'* (What rests, rusts), there is a happy medium of moderate beneficial exercise without risk of injury.

Below are some of the common injuries sustained by joggers.

- Ankle strain is caused by the foot being forced inwards whilst the full body weight is on it. Joggers frequently sustain this injury when running at night down rough tracks and turn the ankle on unseen stones or ruts. The ligaments on the outside of the ankle are torn causing acute pain. Walkers are less likely to suffer this injury than joggers because they have time to adjust their body weight and posture as the foot begins to turn.
- Tenosynovitis of the ankle is a condition in which the

sheath through which the tendon runs across the front of the ankle to the big toe becomes inflamed. The injury is caused by continual and concentrated over-use, such as in jogging for an unaccustomedly long period of time. Burning pain is felt across the foot and alongside the shin.

- Foot strain is particularly common in young men and women who have just left school (where they have spent most of their time seated at desks), and have just started work in a job that requires them to stand for most of the day. The added stress of unaccustomed jogging can cause inflammation of the joints and ligaments that form the ball of the foot causing pain and sometimes swelling.
- Stress fractures result in painful symptoms similar to those experienced with foot strain and therefore it is not easy to diagnose accurately at first. The injury is a hair-line fracture of one of the four long bones in the foot. It is caused by running or marching for long periods on a hard surface like a paved road or pavement. (Sometimes the condition is called 'march fracture'). Diagnosis can only be certain after 4 or 5 weeks when the new bone laid down along the hair-line fracture shows up on an X-ray.
- Tendinitis is a very painful condition caused by inflammation of the Achilles tendon; this is a common complaint of joggers and runners.
- Sprained Knee Ligaments: knee ligaments are prone to strain during twisting falls when the foot becomes jammed between rocks or stuck in a rut. This is another injury easily incurred while jogging at night.
- Knee bursitis is inflammation of the bursae (sacs of lubricating fluid which act as cushions or pads between a tendon and a bone to prevent friction). The painful condition results from persistent pressure or jarring.

What About Aerobics?

At the same time as jogging came under attack, the frenetic fitness work-outs known as aerobics were also being criticised. Aerobics had been promoted in a spate of books written by men and women better known for their achievements in occupations unrelated to medicine or physical education. Helped by ghost writers who could turn a stylish phrase, books on how to look and feel good were turned out with a best-selling imprint, given the 'hype' of a press launch at a glamorous venue, guest appearances by the author on television chat-shows, coast to coast book-signing sessions and 30-foot advertisement hoardings at main-line railway stations. Eventually and inevitably these books found their way onto the half price bargain shelf, their places to be taken by yet another book by a celebrity author presenting another programme for bending, stretching and generally torment-ing the body.

Doctors were appalled by what they read and more so by the sight of the 'victims' who came to their surgeries. 'People are dying as a result of taking badly prescribed exercises,' said Dr Bruce Davies of the Department of Human Kinetics at Salford University. Criticism of these books gathered momentum not only in the professional journals but also in the national press.

A hard-hitting report in *The Times* of 1 September 1986 condemned books and 'work-out' studios which pushed men and women to their limits and welcomed the news that people were now losing interest in such regimes. 'Jane "feel the burn" Fonda, the self-promoted, leotard-clad queen of aerobics and the American fitness movement, appears to be burnt out. The crowds who once attended in their leg-warmers, ballet shoes and leotards have lost their drive.' The article went on to quote frightening statistics from doctors who had investigated the effects of rigorous aerobic sessions.

They derided the Fonda philosophy of 'It's positive pain just like childbirth.' *The Times* report stated: 'Now doctors say extreme exercise by women can cause temporary infertil-ity and spinal bone loss linked to lower oestrogen and calcium levels. A study carried out in California says that injuries are now a major concern of the 27 million American women involved in aerobics: 73 per cent of instructors and 43 per cent of aerobic dancers have suffered minor injuries.'

. The idea of aerobics had originally been planted in the public mind by a book of that title written some twenty years ago by Dr Kenneth Cooper. Now he is reported as saying: 'I've changed my mind. I'm running less and performing better.' Unfortunately those who bought the book are not all aware of this change of mind and many are perhaps still pushing themselves harder than they should. Especially the older ones.

However the present trend among the newer fitness con-verts in Western Europe and America is towards what is surely a more sensible attitude to keeping fit. Men and women today are heeding the warnings and we can all learn from the experience of those who did not. As Dr Sheen said: 'There are days when your body does not want to go out and run. Jim Fixx had the warning signals of chest pain, but he tried to run through them. He should have paid attention to his body, not his mind.'

People were indeed getting hooked on exercise and giving themselves an overdose, especially those who insisted on pushing themselves till it hurt, but fortunately commonsense began to prevail and as the popularity of jogging and aerobics declined a new debate on what kind of exercise might be good for us all gathered momentum.

The Best Exercise

Naturally the merits of swimming and cycling are often described, and they are very good forms of exercise. Swimming is said to exercise every muscle of the body; cycling avoids the strain that running puts on joints yet still provides strenuous exercise for the major leg muscles which comprise two-thirds of the total muscle mass of the body. Both cycling and swimming place demands upon the heart and lungs and so develop the cardio-vascular and respiratory systems. Of this no-one has any doubts.

But neither of these two admirable activities provides comprehensive exercise for the whole body because the muscles are not working against the full force of gravity. Water partially supports the swimmer's body and the cycle frame and wheels bear the weight of the cyclist. Now we know that bones need to be weight-bearing to retain their structural strength: the whole structure of the body, in fact, is modified in accordance with the stresses and strains put upon it. The spongy cancellous tissue within the bone is stimulated to grow along the lines of pressure resulting from the weight of the body. Consequently weight-bearing exercises are essential for comprehensive physical development and fitness.

Walking fits the bill admirably.

Today people of all ages, all classes and all nationalities are discovering for themselves the truth about walking, its many and varied pleasures and its potential for promoting good health. It always has been the most popular of all leisure-time activities, but now studies show that it is the number one exercise activity in America and Western Europe.

One dedicated urban walker, an octagenarian barrister who walks to his Lincoln's Inn Chambers twice a week said, 'Walking is the best life insurance policy you can get.'

Life insurance is an apt description of the protection afforded by the regular habit of walking. And the premiums are not high or demanding. Twenty minutes of brisk walking each day will put you well on the way to a longer life, for walking provides protection against the two major contributors to heart attacks: high blood pressure and obesity.

Such medical evidence, however, is not the only reason that millions of people are now walking far more — especially the urban walkers. There are some interesting factors motivating them to put one foot in front of the other more often every day. These 'buzz factors' — as the marketing men might call the reasons for the upsurge in the popularity of urban walking today — can be clearly identified. They could explain why it is that 90 million Americans are now walking for their physical and psychological well-being and why reports from all the major West European capitals carry the same message.

Why Are They Walking?

Apart from all the benefits of walking as an exercise, it has many unique advantages over other forms of exercise which no doubt contribute to its increasing popularity with both urban and country walkers. Some of these are listed below.

- It's so simple and safe. Walking is a natural activity, no introductory lessons are needed. To join the cult of serious walkers all you need to do is to increase your pace gradually and progressively; lengthen the distance you walk every day.
- Almost anyone can do it. The young and the old, male and female, the fit and the not so fit can all benefit.
- No special skill or equipment is needed. Apart from comfortable footwear (more about this later) and ordinary protective clothing to guard against the effects of cold and of hot sun, nothing else is needed. No expensive racquets or other expensive equipment are required.
- You can do it almost anywhere. You can walk along almost any pavement or street starting just outside your own front

door. You can step out inconspicuously without any of the embarrassment that many older joggers feel as they turn out in their shorts or jogging kit. The variety of routes and settings available makes walking an enormously pleasurable activity.

● You can do it at almost any time. You don't have to find a partner. Walking works easily into the daily routine and requires hardly any preparation.

● Everyone says how much better they feel for it. Nothing works better than word of mouth recommendation. It reinforces your own resolve to do more fitness walking.

● All benefits are absolutely free! No club membership fees are required before you can become a walker and you save money on rail, bus or car costs.

Rewards of Walking

There are many kinds of walking: walking out with a girl- or boy-friend, taking the dog for a walk, walking round the shops, walking over the fells and even a short walk through the Hindu Kush. There is tramping, hiking, rambling, strolling and, of course, walking to work.

Doctors have already advocated walking as a sensible form of exercise that can pave the way to a better life; now they are being more specific and recommending *fitness walking*. All this means is that you walk briskly enough to raise your heart and respiration rate to a level higher than normal. This will promote a healthy development of the heart, lungs and circulatory system generally. For most people the speed for fitness walking would be about 3–4½ miles an hour. The rate depends upon your age and state of fitness, but we shall go into the details of speed and distances later.

There was a time when walking was not seriously regarded as a purposeful exercise activity for keeping fit. Somehow it was too easy. There was no real sweat and certainly no pain. Now that attitude has disappeared and walking has gained accolades from all sides of the medical, scientific and physical education professions. Recent studies show that the rewards from regular fitness walking can equal and even exceed those from running and other aerobic activities. Indeed, many sports specialists regard fitness walking as one of the best ways of achieving aerobic fitness; it can greatly improve the body's ability to utilise oxygen during physical activity, re-

duce the resting heart rate, lower blood pressure and generally increase the efficiency of the heart and lungs. This increased efficiency gives you stamina, staying power or the
ability to keep going without gasping for breath.

With walking however — as with any new exercise routine
— it is important to go easy at first and build up gradually.
The philosophy recommended by the medical profession is
to err on the side of 'under-doing' it rather than over-doing it.

Perhaps the best advice to those new to walking would be
that given by one of the most loved of walkers and writers of
all time, George Borrow. He was a man who wandered
everywhere, in Russia, Portugal, Spain, Ireland, Wales and
many other countries. He mastered twenty languages, loved
horseflesh, boxing, and fairs, and many a time covered 50 or
60 miles on foot between dawn and sunset.

Borrow advised all who walked and exercised in any way
to take heed of messages sent by the body and to progress
slowly. 'Pain of any sort is Nature's danger signal. We only
come to grief when we neglect or misunderstand it.' He
urged beginners at walking to remember the fable of Milo,
the celebrated Pythagorean wrestler and walker. One night a
calf was born on his father's farm and in the morning Milo
walked up the hill to the cowshed, picked up the calf and
carried it fondly around. He did this every morning as the
weeks passed and the calf grew bigger. But each morning it
required just a little bit more effort and Milo's muscles were
taxed just a fraction more every day. But his muscles developed to cope with the task of lifting the growing calf and
carrying it up the hill. At last, the persevering young man
could be seen lightly springing up the hillside with a full-
sized ox on his shoulder.

We can get through life without having to lift young oxen,
but who can get through life without any walking? And the
more developed the walking muscles are then the more we
can do without feeling fatigue. We can finish the day's work
fresh and with energy to spare for other activities, for leisure,
for family and friends. We must never forget that the time for
enjoying ourselves is *now* and the place, *here*. If your walking
muscles atrophy and waste away with disuse then the whole
body becomes progressively weaker. It makes sense to give
walking your fullest attention, but to enjoy all the benefits of
walking it is essential to make it part of your life rather than
an activity you indulge in now and again, when you think

you have some free time. Everyone can make time for walking, especially those who travel some distance to work each day, for they can make part of the journey on foot.

For them the 'walking work-out' can become a pleasurable health-promoting routine.

2

Walking Works Wonders

'These men I have examined around the world who live in vigorous health to 100 or more years are great walkers. If you want to live a long long time in sturdy health you can't go wrong in forming the habit of walking every day . . . until it becomes a habit as important as eating and sleeping.'

Dr Leaf, *Executive Health Organisation*, California

The radio alarm went off at 7.00 am with the BBC morning news. Margaret Duffield, obeying movements long since grooved into a ritual, stretched out fully, pulled the flannelette sheet up around her neck and sank into billows of luxury making herself a present of the most pleasurable 10 minutes of the day.

'My life,' she thought, as she stared upwards at the dusty basket-work lampshade, 'is essentially just what it was 5 years ago when my husband left me with two young daughters to raise. But then I was able to bound out of bed with energy enough to meet the challenges of the day; getting the girls ready for the school bus before driving to work myself.'

Where had all that energy gone now? She was not yet 40 years old and yet she felt tired before the day had even started. Then she chanced to hear an item on the morning news that changed her life. The presenter was saying: 'A Surrey journalist, Helen Krasner, has just completed the longest continuous walk ever done by a woman. She has walked right round the coast of Britain. Setting off from Brighton on 1 March 1986 she returned yesterday (31 January 1987) having completed a clockwise walk of more than 4922 miles (7921 km).'

Margaret Duffield heard no more of that news bulletin: ideas were tumbling about in her head. 'Suddenly without any conscious effort,' she recalled, 'I'd made up my mind. I was going to walk more myself. Not more than Helen Krasner, but more than I usually did. Every day. To reinforce this spontaneous decision I took out my diary and put a star on the day. Each day after that I recorded systematically the distance I had walked. My aim was to increase the distance each week. Sometimes, as the weekend approached, I had to go out for a quick nip around the block before going to bed to make sure I should reach my weekly target in my own record book. It might seem a bit of a fag but it's certainly been worth the effort. I sleep better, get up livelier, feel more confident, and I've definitely packed more living into the day than ever before.'

Earn a Bonus

Margaret Duffield's experience is not unique. There is some magic about walking that triggers off countless extra benefits, and enriches life. The process of living has many dimensions and one of the most important of these is obviously its length. But apart from the number of years, there is also the quality of life to consider, and what Margaret Duffield discovered was that she became more alert and sensitively alive when she took up exercise walking. Now she no longer has a tough time getting out of bed in the morning. No longer is she dragged down by the demands of being a working single parent coping with a classroom full of kids by day and a living room full at night. Now she takes everything literally in her stride! The brisk walk to school gives her time to unwind from the early morning breakfast rush, and the walk home is equally relaxing and energising at the same time. This might seem a contradiction in terms to those who have not experienced the feeling.

At weekends now she takes a longer 18 mile walk from Southern Down along the Welsh coast by Nash Point to St Athan. By the time she gets home she has worked out all the problems a single parent accumulates during a week. Walking works wonders.

There is no need for punishing aerobic routines. As Professor Morehouse writes in his book *Total Fitness*: 'Better to be content with taking a little walk every day than to join a jogging group you know you don't belong in. That's why I advocate an exercise programme that isn't too tough to take. Your heart must be in it.'

As we have already seen, thousands of men and women are now turning away from the more rigorous forms of physical exercise and taking to walking.

'Urban walking is right up my street, if you'll excuse the pun,' said accountant John Kerrigan, a short-necked, rotund man who always wears braces because there is no place for a belt to grip where his waist ought to be. 'Nobody would ever get me into a track suit prancing about in a gym. I know I need to exercise, but I know also that I would never stick at it and would do only the bare minimum. But now I walk whenever I can instead of driving or taking a bus. I have to move about the city a fair bit in my job and now I'm used to the idea of walking and find that it saves me both time and money.'

It could also save him a lot more. His life. With that kind of figure he is a classic candidate for heart trouble.

For Your Heart's Sake, Walk!

We are all now familiar with the frightening figures relating to heart disease. More than one million Americans suffer a heart attack each year and more than half of them die before they reach hospital. The British have a greater incidence of heart attacks than all other Europeans.

These figures are so familiar that we no longer think of them as we should — as a horrifying and avoidable epidemic. There is no reason why we should accept heart disease as inevitable. We can take action to protect ourselves from the degenerative changes that affect the circulatory system.

These changes have various causes: smoking, eating a fatty diet, excessive stress, hypertension, diabetes, obesity and lack of physical exercise. Most of the factors which increase the risk of heart attacks can be alleviated by regular walking.

The beneficial effects of walking were listed for us by Dr Samuel Fox, a former President of the American College of Cardiology. He believes brisk walking can help our cardio-vascular and respiratory system by:

- opening a greater number of blood vessels in muscular tissues;
- improving the resilience of blood vessels, making them more elastic and consequently less prone to rupture;

15

- developing neuro-muscular control and increasing the size of muscle fibres, thereby improving the efficiency of muscles in utilising oxygen in the bloodstream;
- increasing the size and power of the heart muscle so that its stroke/volume is increased and more blood is being pumped around the body with each beat;
- increasing cardiac reserve so that the heart is better able to cope with sudden extreme demands made upon it in emergencies;
- reducing blood pressure thus reducing the risk of heart attacks;
- reducing harmful cholesterol levels thus lowering the risk of fats being deposited in the arteries.

The Cholesterol Factor

Although cholesterol is a controversial subject, a large body of medical opinion backs the theory that regular exercise such as walking can have a beneficial effect upon levels of cholesterol in the bloodstream.

Scarcely a day goes by without our hearing of some risk from cholesterol and most people are aware of that fearsome fatty substance which might thicken the walls of our arteries. This is not surprising because dramatic press reports in recent years have highlighted the risk of heart attacks associated with a raised blood-cholesterol level. But the full story of cholesterol is rarely told.

Cholesterol is not all that most of us think it is. Nor does it just come from eating harmful and fatty foods. The picture is far more complex than that.

Surprisingly, most of the cholesterol in our bloodstreams does not originate from what we have eaten at all. It is already there having been made by our own body — mostly in the liver. It may be news to many readers that only 15 per cent of cholesterol in the bloodstream actually comes from our diet. This might make us think again about the whole problem.

Doctors explain the situation in this way: 'Even cutting your cholesterol intake dramatically has only a minor effect on the overall level. The reason for this is that the body goes on making cholesterol no matter how much cholesterol your diet contains. Excess dietary cholesterol is merely eliminated via the excretory system.'

But don't think you can go back to your fatty diet with

impunity, for before we can decide what to do about the cholesterol problem there is more we need to know. First we have to realise that there are two kinds of cholesterol — high-density lipoprotein cholesterol (HDL) and low-density lipoprotein cholesterol (LDL). The HDL actually protects the body against heart attacks. The advice doctors give is that we should aim to increase the ratio of HDL to LDL. The best way of achieving this is through changes in the diet and through exercise which has some effect in increasing the HDL cholesterol.

To sum up then, what you can do to avoid problems with cholesterol is:

● Lower your intake of all kinds of fats and cut down drastically on saturated fats which encourage the liver to produce large amounts of cholesterol.
● Walk for 20–30 minutes a day on four or five days of the week. Studies show that such a walking programme would significantly raise the beneficial HDL level of cholesterol in two months.
● Avoid stress and relax whenever you can. Bouts of excessive stress can cause the liver to discharge sugar into the bloodstream to provide muscles with extra energy, and there may also be an excessive release of cholesterol.

For a Longer Life

Regular, safe walking can reverse the degenerative changes that come with premature ageing. Research into the detail of life-styles of 5,000 men who died in Boston during 1969 produced evidence about such factors as smoking, obesity, hours of sleep, and physical recreation taken during leisure hours and work. All these factors were then analysed to see whether they were correlated with the length of life of the men studied.

The predominant factor affecting longevity was the time spent in physical recreation and walking during leisure time. The severity of the daily manual work did not seem to affect the general pattern at all. The men who played games and walked lived an average of 11 years longer than others.

But though you can walk to a longer, fuller life, you cannot expect walking on its own to counteract abuse of the body, for example by smoking, stress, and over-eating. Fortunately, however, once you start walking more, you adopt a more healthy life-style and take action to reduce the adverse influence of previous harmful habits on health.

Walking produces a beneficial 'knock-on' effect. You will feel better, look forward to the enjoyment of your daily urban walks, and because of the pleasurable feeling that it brings, you will do more of it, get more enjoyment, feel fitter and stand a better chance of extending your life expectancy.

Banishing Fatigue

Fit people look younger, feel livelier and have stamina enough to finish the day's work comfortably and still feel fresh enough to enjoy their leisure. They are the people who get things done. Seldom do they feel fatigued as they go from one activity to the next. Anatole France was surely right when he wrote: 'Man is so made that he can find relaxation from one kind of labour by taking up another. You can feel tired perhaps after work, but you can still enjoy walking for it immediately gives you that feeling of relaxation and freedom as soon as you step away from the office or from the home.'

Fatigue never bothers active people. Perhaps this is because the phenomenon of fatigue is brought on by a combination of factors, psychological as well as physical. There is the fatigue that comes from vigorous muscular activity producing oxygen debt and the waste products of physiological fatigue which have to be disperced. There is also the fatigue brought on by mental conditions of frustration, boredom, stress and anxiety. Walking can relieve fatigue from all these causes. Strange though it may seem, exercise can actually generate a fresh supply of energy.

Men and women are now finding that after a hard day's work in the office or workshop, a brisk walk on the way home enables them to arrive feeling livelier than if they had ridden all the way. Travelling in crowded trains can bring on fatigue as a result of poor air conditioning, which tends to cause dehydration. When very dry air circulates in the ventilating system it can cause the loss of water which produces feelings of fatigue accompanied by other physical symptoms such as flushing, dry skin and mucous membranes, cracked lips, low blood pressure and lethargy. You feel generally under par. This feeling, which is similar to the feeling of jet lag, can be relieved by a brisk walk after the journey. For this reason it would be worth trying the experiment of leaving the commuting train or bus a stop or two earlier than your usual one. You will soon notice the difference not only in your pocket, but also in the way that you feel when you reach home. You might also find there are further benefits which you had not expected. As Paul Garland did.

Improving Sexual Performance

'I used to run out of steam by four or five o'clock,' said Paul, a 41 year old inspector of taxes. 'By the time that I got home, had a meal and watched the news on TV I was invariably asleep. After taking to walking more I've taken up other things too — a night class in German and another in ballroom dancing.'

His wife, with a wicked twinkle in her eye, added, 'I've never known him do so much around the house either; tiling the bathroom and' (here giving him a playful dig in the ribs), 'he's much better in bed.'

She could be right. 'Faced with increasing pressure at the office, in the home, and in the bedroom, some men turn away from women,' says Dr Andrew Stanway in his book 'A Woman's Guide to Men and Sex' (Century, 1988). But one of the immediate effects of being totally fit is an improvement in sexual performance. A specialist in this field, Professor Laurence Morehouse, writes: 'If you're fatigued and flabby, your response will match your physical state. Perhaps one of the most demanding aspects of sex from a physiological point of view is that it produces an elevated heart rate and blood pressure. If you're out of shape your performance will suffer.'

One of the most obvious signs of being 'out of shape' is an overwhelming feeling of fatigue and lethargy. This in itself can put anyone off sex resulting in the 'not tonight, I've got a headache' syndrome. Men may worry about impotence; there is no need for this worry.

A team of specialist doctors who studied the physical and mental pressures which led people at the top of their professions into a state of exhaustion and impaired sexual function published their findings in the BMA *Book of Executive Health* (Tunes Books, 1979) had this to say: 'Fatigue is often to blame for poor sexual performance and male impotence. The vast majority of men with impotence have no detectable disease and most are amenable to treatment.'

Women may also suffer from a variety of gynaecological disorders but they too respond to therapy and to walking.

It is important to see the problem in its proper perspective. Nearly half of all married couples, it is said, (in BUPA's *Manual of Fitness and Well-Being*, Macdonald, 1984) have some sexual difficulties at some time and the first step along the road to putting life back into an ailing sex life could be one that you can literally take yourself. Walk more, enjoy more active leisure and get fit. Walking banishes fatigue.

Obviously, more therapy than simply walking may be needed before all sexual problems are solved, for they arise from a subtle and complex mixture of psychological causes. And they do not develop overnight, but could well be the result of partners letting their sex life lapse into a stale routine, taking everything for granted.

Partners must be frank with each other, express their dissatisfaction honestly, but in a way that is not harmful. What better way could there be of beginning such a dialogue than in taking an evening walk together. It would provide opportunities for airing feelings and talking candidly. The exercise in itself would have an uplifting effect mentally as well as physically. Remember that physical exercise is the flywheel that sets in motion all the other body systems — digestive, nervous, endocrine, circulatory, respiratory and reproductive — making them all the more efficient. It really can banish fatigue. It gives you the attractive glow of physical fitness and the lively manner of those with energy to spare.

With that extra energy there comes a feeling of confidence and a new concept of sexuality. When you feel better about yourself you send out more effective signals to others which bring pleasing responses. *These signals are sex appeal!*

Confidence

It doesn't matter whether you walk every day in the city or whether you take time off and walk round the coastline of Britain, walking gives you a great feeling of confidence. Let one of those who has experienced this explain. In an interview with the writer Helen Krasner explained that she was 'between jobs' when she decided to take a long walk. 'I'd never done anything like it before, but I just took it into my head to walk right round Britain before starting work again.'

'Early March was perhaps not the best of times to start, but I didn't know how long it would take me and at least I had the milder months of Spring, Summer and Autumn ahead, or so I thought. The first thing I had to learn was how much my body would take and in those first three weeks I learnt a lot.

'Walking alone gave me time to think and be aware of my own physical capabilities, not just in walking but in enduring conditions of cold, biting winds, lashing rain. The very first night that I put up my little bivouac tent there was a tremendous storm; it was as if I was going to be put through a testing period during those first three weeks, but at the end of them I began to realise that I could cope well enough and that all those people who had tried to put me off were wrong. There's nothing like the success of achievement, no matter how small, for building up self-confidence. And as the walk went on and I grew more aware of what my body could and could not do I grew as a person and began to feel much better mentally and physically.'

Helen Krasner's boots wore out after 2,000 miles of walking an average of 17 miles every day, but by this time nothing would stop her, not breaking in a new pair of boots nor coping with a crop of boils for which the doctor advised a few days' rest. Helen Krasner had discovered herself, she knew she could carry on, but she also knew that if she once stopped she might never start again. 'Keep going and take every day as it comes,' was her philosophy.

The urban walker could profit from that advice. Start with achievable aims and then keep going. There are various devices which other urban walkers have found useful, to help you with such a resolution. (See Chapter 3.)

Muscular Development

Walking helps to tone up and strengthen the whole muscular system and especially the muscles of the legs which comprise two-thirds of the total muscle mass of the body. It is also good for those muscles affecting posture.

It is easy to see how walking develops the skeletal muscles, but what is not always so easy to comprehend is the way that walking strengthens the heart muscle. It does this just as surely as would the exercise from what might be considered the more taxing exercises — jogging or aerobics.

In addition, walking which develops the leg muscles can

give you a stronger 'second heart' and for this urban walking is just as effective, if not more so, than long distance walking. Doctors explain the phenomenon of the 'second heart' in this way. When the muscles of the leg contract (those in the feet, calves, thighs and buttocks), they exert a rhythmical squeezing pressure upon the veins and smaller blood vessels in the leg thus forcing the blood onwards towards the heart against the pull of gravity. This squeezing action greatly helps the heart in its daily task of pushing 18,000 gallons of blood round the body. The second heart muscles work most effectively when you walk.

A Better Circulatory System

Judith and Heather Robinson are sisters who work in a big Newcastle department store. They have been sales assistants since leaving school. Now they are nearing their forties, and recently, for the first time in their lives, they went to see a doctor. There was nothing seriously wrong with their health, but each of them had discovered, during a tea-break chat, that they were both finding bumps and bulges on veins sticking out in a worrying manner on the inside of their knees and on the calves of their legs. They were in fact now paying the price of years of standing for long hours daily — varicose veins.

Such abnormally dilated and knotted-looking blood vessels lying close to the surface of the skin are especially common in people whose work necessitates long periods of standing with little walking. Blood has to travel upwards to reach the heart, and at intervals in the veins there are valves which prevent the blood from flowing backwards with the pull of gravity. In some people these valves become weak from carrying the load of blood for hours on end without any help from the leg muscles to squeeze it upwards. Varicose veins can become painful if neglected, but fortunately these two women sought help in time. They rested whenever they could, supported the veins with special stockings whilst at work and they took to walking more often. They too joined the ranks of the urban walker.

'I used to say I was on my feet enough without taking exercise or walking more than I should,' said Judith, 'but now I do walk more and have had no more painful veins.'

Leg muscles are very important in helping the heart to do

its job. Doctors now advise heart patients to walk more often so that the lower leg muscles can take on a fair share of work in circulating the blood. Even a few minutes walking at intervals during the day helps the heart and costs little effort. Once again it is something everyone can do. A quick walk around your office block can work wonders in so many ways.

Avoiding Brittle Bones

Accidents will happen. Bones will be broken and they are likely to be broken more often as you grow older. But you can guard against this possibility by keeping your bones structurally strong. Walking strengthens bones and helps to retard bone loss or bone thinning (osteoporosis), a condition in which bones lose part of their protein framework (matrix) and this leads to brittleness. Men can be affected, but the condition is more prevalent in women. As many as 25 per cent of postmenopausal women are afflicted.

The cause of osteoporosis may be a dietary deficiency, particularly of calcium; it may be. lack of use, as with a paralysed limb or following severe wounds to muscle tissue; or it may be associated with a reduction in the amount of sex hormones such as occurs after menopause. But the primary cause is inactivity. Bones need to be functional, active and above all, weight-bearing.

Walking has a beneficial effect upon all the bones of the body and particularly on all the articulated vertebrae which flex to enable them bear the body weight with each walking step and transfer it downwards to the pelvic girdle, thigh bones, shin bones and all the 26 bones of the feet. These bones act as a platform upon which the whole body weight is then balanced. To function efficiently all bones need to be strong and healthy. They need food and exercise. Calcium-rich foods such as sardines, skimmed milk, yoghurt, salmon with bones, spinach, broccoli, oranges, cheese and corn muffins will provide the essential nutrients required by the bones.

Walking will do the rest.

Breath-Taking

There are a lot of exercise purveyors out there offering you all sorts of deals that will improve the efficiency of your heart and lungs. But walking is as natural as breathing and it can improve heart/lung function to a degree that will help you through the day with minimal fatigue.

It is the urban walker who walks daily who will achieve the best results, as we shall see. Brisk walking has the capacity for raising aerobic fitness levels without the pain and punishment of the more violent forms of exercise. As Dr James Rippe, a cardiologist and clinical director of the University of Massachusetts Medical Centre for Health and Fitness affirms in *The Walkways Almanac* (Walkways Center Inc. and Rockport Company Washington DC, 1987).

> People are sometimes surprised to learn that walking can be an aerobic form of exercise because it seems so easy. You don't have to have sweat pouring down your brow to achieve benefit from an aerobic exercise. Both a high-class athlete and the average person can achieve enough exercise from fitness walking to derive the maximum benefit to their hearts. *Very simply, fitness walking is the best exercise for conditioning the vast majority of people.*

Physical fitness is like money in a way: you have to work regularly to earn it. But in another way it is not like money — you can't bank fitness. 'Deterioration in fitness can be detected after only three days in bed,' say British Medical Association doctors who have studied the health of executives in their book, 'Executive Health' (Times Publishing, 1979)

There is little point therefore in undertaking a fitness programme unless there is a will and an opportunity to continue with at least three 20-minute sessions every week. How many of our would-be sporting enthusiasts could tackle such a programme for more than a few weeks?

But the urban walker is at it every day!

Brisk walking can get the heart working up to 70–80 per cent of its capacity and will increase the respiration rate correspondingly. As a result, the lungs develop to cope with the tasks presented to them. During exercise, additional oxygen and energy fuel are required and lactic acid and carbon dioxide are formed. In order to provide more oxygen and to eliminate carbon dioxide, the rate and depth of respiration increase, thus exposing a greater area of the lungs for the interchange of gases. The increase in rate and depth of

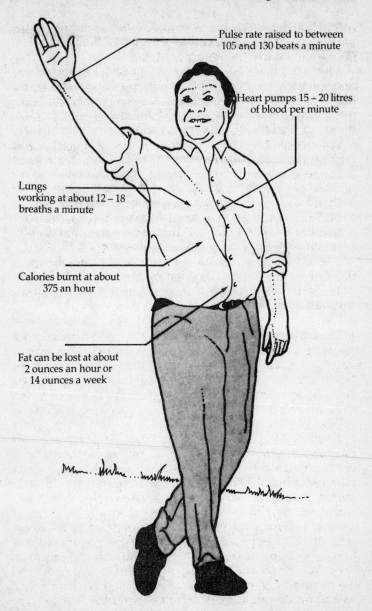

Pulse rate raised to between
105 and 130 beats a minute

Heart pumps 15 – 20 litres
of blood per minute

Lungs
working at about 12 – 18
breaths a minute

Calories burnt at about
375 an hour

Fat can be lost at about
2 ounces an hour or
14 ounces a week

Fig.1.   What happens when a man weighing 180 pounds walks at
3½ m.p.h.?

respiration is entirely reflexive and results mainly from the greater concentration of carbon dioxide in the blood acting chemically on the respiratory centre of the brain.

After a few weeks of regular brisk walking the normal rate of respiration decreases. The average rate of respiration for a man who is not in good condition is normally about 20 times a minute, whereas the fit athlete may only breathe in eight times per minute, for the same amount of muscular activity.

With regular exercise walking the vital capacity (the volume of air the lungs can breathe in and out) increases so that a greater area of lung surface can be presented to the inspired air. This means that a greater volume of gases can be exchanged in the same breath. Experiments have shown that fit men and women will breathe in less air for the same amount of work than those who are not so fit, indicating a more efficient system for absorbing oxygen.

The urban walker who takes a 15- or 20-minute walk twice a day can greatly improve respiratory efficiency and thus the potential for doing long periods of exhaustive work requiring respiratory stamina.

Walking certainly works wonders. Now it's time to get your programme started.

3

The Urban Walker's Work-out

'Feel fitter, trimmer, healthier in 30 days or your money back. Get into great shape with this fun exerciser. It does wonders for your legs, tummy and general fitness. Just a few minutes each day will tone up your muscles. You'll enjoy improved vitality. You'll look better. Feel better. Fast.'

So runs a full-page advertisement in a Sunday newspaper's colour supplement for an exercise device claiming it to be the best all-round exerciser that money can buy. How many of us have similar devices in the attic or lumber room? Apparatus that promised to slim hips, trim the paunch, cure back-ache and many other defects.

The copy-writer's blurb is effective, it appeals to anyone who realises that they are not doing enough exercise and wants an easy, embarrassment-free way back to physical fitness. As a token of intention it is easy enough to write a cheque and send off for the machine. It eases the conscience for a while until the postman brings the product to the door. Then exercise can be put off no longer. And then? Well we know what happens. Eventually such a device gathers dust in a corner until it appears either in the small miscellaneous sales advertisements in the local free press or is simply pushed somewhere out of sight.

When you come to think harder about the above sales blurb, you realise that exactly the same words could be used for the most effective, easiest, and certainly the cheapest, work-out of them all — urban walking.

What, you might ask, makes a walk a 'work-out'?

Essentials of a Physical Conditioning Programme

The fundamental principles of any 'work-out' are that the programme should:

- meet the needs of the individual — young or old, fit or unfit, male or female;
- be safe but effective;
- be graded to ensure steady but sure progress;
- provide exercise which improves cardio-vascular respiratory efficiency;
- burn calories as energy fuel;
- provide an easy means of monitoring progress so that you always work within safe limits;
- foster motivation for further effort from the satisfaction derived from a tangible improvement in physical ability.

The urban walker's work-out meets all these requirements. It is largely a matter of pace, distance and progression. There are guidelines to follow which will help everyone to achieve maximum improvement with minimum expenditure of time and effort.

Since aerobics and jogging took the world by storm and then quietly faded from the scene, the exercisers now arousing all the interest are the urban walkers. They are not easy to recognise for they come in various guises. But they are not the traditional commuter, nor the shopper, not the strolling rubber-necked tourist. They are a different breed of pedestrian altogether.

They do not take to the roads in skimpy tops of lycra or cotton jersey matched with shorts or leggings that finish anywhere from below the knee to above the ankle, nor colourfully banded legwarmers wrinkling round the ankles: they don't even wear track suits.

Quietly and systematically they are having a daily 'work-out' just as effective if not more so than jogging or aerobics. Their aims are modest at first and not like those of followers of the manic aerobic cult which were often set far too high. The progression of the urban walker is more realistic and consequently there are fewer drop-outs.

Gently does it.

Naturally urban walkers do not saunter, stroll or shuffle along the pavements and streets, but they start at a steady clip and work up to a brisk pace — demanding enough to make the heart beat faster and the breathing deeper. The beginner should aim to put an increasing demand upon the cardio-vascular system.

Is Walking Aerobic Exercise?

When, in the early 1960s, Dr Kenneth Cooper, a cardiologist, was given the task of keeping American airmen and astronauts fit, he devised a programme of physical exercise which made sufficient demands upon the heart and lungs to develop functional efficiency. He called these exercises 'aerobics'.

The principle of putting increasing demands upon the heart and lungs was adapted in many ways — in dance studios, exercise gyms, in jogging, swimming and cycling. Points were awarded for periods spent in certain activities or 'work-out' sessions.

Walking can be adapted to meet all the criteria of an aerobic exercise.

Look at it this way. The basic output of the heart is 4–5 litres of blood per minute. During rigorous exercise the maximum output might reach 40 litres a minute, of which nearly 1 litre goes to the heart muscle itself.

As the walking pace is increased there is a corresponding increase in depth and rate of respiration. At first these increases are rapid. You can tell immediately whether you are making adequate demands or not. The initial increase is followed by a slower, but gradual, rise to the final maximum rate of respiration.

How can you tell if your walking pace is putting too much or too little strain on the system? A good guide is whether or not you could carry on a conversation as you walk. If you can't talk without becoming breathless you are going too fast.

This simple rule tells you if your walking pace has pushed your heart rate above the safe target zone for your age and physical condition. Study the heart rate chart on page 35 and you will see that to maintain your target heart rate you will need to walk at a pace of 3–4 miles an hour, so that your target heart rate is at about 60–85 per cent of your maximum heart rate. (Consultants for the US President's Council on Physical Fitness and Health, 1986.)

But irrespective of these figures, the basic guide is to listen to what your body is telling you. Heed any warning of breathlessness or nausea: slow down if this happens. Progress will come in time. Don't push yourself further if you have a pounding heart thinking you will be doing yourself good. You won't. All you will succeed in doing is arriving home or at the office in a distressed state which might put you off walking altogether.

The point cannot be stressed too much. Today the 'buzz phrase' for exercise, in the light of recent medical research, is 'low-impact'.

Getting Started

'A journey of 1,000 miles begins with a single step', is a saying we've all heard. And that first step is going to make walking a part of your life. Not just something you do now and again, but every day so that it is integrated pleasurably with your work, leisure, and social activities. Even shopping, a tedious activity for some, can be used satisfyingly to clock up more miles for your record book.

We all know basically what we want to achieve; a highly efficient, great-looking, active body and an alert mind. We know also how easy it is to start a new activity and how difficult it is to keep going. It is for this reason that walking is going to be more than just another of those 'keep fit' phases. It really is going to be part of your life for it is an activity that is going to be accessible to you through all your years. In your younger days it will build up your basic body strength and later on will help to protect your body from the ravages of degenerative diseases.

In any case, most of us will not get through life without some walking so it is important to make sure that our bones and walking muscles are strong enough for a lifetime's work. Therefore, that first step must be just right.

Do not start too ambitiously so that you find yourself too stiff and tired to carry on the next day. You have a long time ahead to make progress, so walk to your training pulse level as shown on the chart (page 37). Never push yourself to excessive fatigue.

Increase your oxygen intake by walking just a little faster when you feel up to it, and a little further without straining yourself. Gradually you will improve your cardio-vascular and respiratory efficiency. Your stamina and general fitness will develop in ways that will surprise you.

Making Progress

The most vulnerable weeks once you have started the walking way to fitness will be the first few, during which the habit of daily walking is just becoming ingrained and integrated into your daily routine.

Give yourself a chance to ease into the programme gradually. Make a commitment and stick with it. There are no short cuts to be taken. Often a friend, equally committed, will help you to keep a regular progressive programme. Also, the very act of logging your walks daily on a record chart will help; note the progress in terms of distances, times, paces and any increase in degree of difficulty in the walks such as weight carried, or change in route involving walking up steeper roads.

In order to give you a more accurate idea of your progress in urban walking keep a record of your pulse rate at certain fixed points of the walk. When you exercise, your heart beats faster according to the intensity of that exercise. And as you become fitter your heart muscle becomes stronger and the beats become more regular and slower.

What has happened is that the increase in size and strength of the heart muscle enables it to pump a greater volume of blood into the arteries with each beat; its stroke volume is raised. Consequently the resting heart rate drops. The resting heart rate of a very fit long distance fell walker, for example, might be as low as 45 beats to the minute whereas that of the untrained, but healthy person may be between 60 and 70 beats per minute.

The same sort of reaction has been found in animals — the more active ones have larger hearts than those that don't run about so much. Greyhounds, for example, have larger hearts than pet house dogs of the same size.

The enlarged heart, satisfying normal requirements with a slow resting beat, has greater reserve (cardiac reserve) to call upon when the demands of increased exertion need to be met by an increase in blood-flow. What it all amounts to is that a heart with a low rate of beating gives you more power with less effort.

As a rough guide, the resting pulse rate is a good indication of your overall condition, but if you would like a more accurate test of your physical fitness, then certain organisations or your own physician could arrange for you to have an exercise-stress test. You will be wired up for recordings of your heart, and will have to breathe into a mouthpiece whilst walking on a motorised treadmill. By looking at the cardiogram while the heart is under stress, the physician can tell how fit your heart is and the progress you have made. For most purposes, however, the lowering of the resting pulse rate is a sound enough indication of progress being made towards optimum fitness.

Some people might have difficulty in taking their own pulse. You can take it at the wrist by placing the first two fingers of your right hand on the radial artery of the inner wrist of the left hand, in the gap that you can feel between bone and ligaments just below the base of the thumb. Count the number of beats in 15 seconds (or 30) and multiply by four (or two if you count for 30 seconds) to obtain the rate per minute. Your walking record chart should show the resting pulse rate, the rate after 10 minutes walking, the rate when you finish the walk and the rate after 5 minutes sitting. This final reading will show your recovery rate which is another good indication of your state of fitness. The figures will also tell you if you are giving yourself a satisfactory work-out or not, and the progress you have made.

You will soon find that walking can give you a work-out that will tax the heart, lungs and circulatory system as severely as you need, but obviously, for balanced muscular development a few supplementary conditioning exercises will be necessary. We shall look at these later. (Chapter 9.)

Now here is something that will bolster the resolve of any reader who might still have doubts about the value of daily urban walking. It's a fact which might be difficult to accept were if not for the statistical evidence from the results of a rigorous scientific test. It is this: walking, despite its low intensity aspect, is an activity which has an aerobic effect almost as great as jogging or the 'aerobics work-outs'. It has also been found that a person who weighs 150 pounds and walks at between 3 and 4 miles an hour for 8 hours will use over 3500 calories. This is said to be more calories than a good runner will use during a 26-mile marathon!

But you don't have to walk for 8 hours at once. The urban walkers can clock up their hours steadily each day as their legs take them down the road to increased vitality and good health.

Naturally each individual will have different objectives to reach on his walk to physical well-being and everyone will be starting from different situations, according to age and physical condition. If you have not been exercising for some months or years, and feel out of condition, then set yourself a pace of no more than 3 miles an hour and see how your heart responds. If your pulse rate is still above your target zone then slow down, you are overdoing it. But if your heart rate at the end of the first 5 or 10 minutes is below your target zone then you have not been walking vigorously enough to achieve a worthwhile effect upon your cardio-vascular system.

A good tip for anyone beginning an urban walking programme is to take a car ride around your walking area and use the speedometer to measure distances between well-known landmarks. If you walk in the city near your place of work then it would perhaps be better to take a trip into the area at night or at the weekend when the streets are less congested with traffic. If you have a list of distances in your record book you will be more likely to make progress with your work-out. Keep a weekly record of what you have done, how far you have walked and for how long.

Be businesslike. You are managing the most important thing in your life — your health.

One sure way to get yourself in the walking habit is to make sure that you *do* walk a significant distance every day. You can start very modestly, but as long as you make some progress daily or weekly you are bound to succeed in making walking with all its benefits an essential part of your life. Regularity is important. Do not let the weather put you off.

Below is a simple chart for your record book. Keep one like it handy in your bedroom or living room, so that by seeing it open waiting for your daily report you are frequently reminded of the need to walk.

In the comments column you might remark upon the route followed, the weather and the time. Comments on the gradients and track or path surface are pertinent ones too, for walking along a rough but level road uses about 50 per cent more energy than walking on a pavement. And, of course, walking uphill can take as much as four times more than the effort needed to walk along a level route. Even downhill walking is more energy-consuming than walking along the flat, for in going downhill the legs are working in a propelling and breaking action almost at the same time.

Keeping a check on your walking performance will give you motivation in the same way that having yourself weighed weekly by the Weight Watchers' tutor would help

The Walking Chart

Date Started _____   Weight _____

Resting Pulse Rate _____

Date	Route	Conditions underfoot Weather	General remarks	Time/ Pace	Distance

Weekly distance

Aims for following week:

Aims and objectives for next week:

Improvement over previous week

you to succeed in working off the pounds at a steady rate.

One final word about your walking progress. There is a 'spin-off' bonus. Progress does not come merely in terms of physical development due to exercise, it comes also from a curious side-effect influencing all the other factors which affect fitness. The interesting point about walking is that it generates an awareness of all these factors and few people are going to undermine the efforts they have put in on the roads and pavements by failing to observe a sensible attitude towards diet, alcohol and smoking. Thus, the physical improvement that comes with walking builds enthusiasm for a positive attitude towards healthy living. Very quickly the convert to walking begins to enjoy the exhilaration that comes with it and wakes up in the morning feeling refreshed and full of vitality.

Setting Your Walking Pace to Suit Your State of Fitness

Set a target zone for your heart rate according to your age. That is, 220 beats a minute minus your age. Thus, at age 40 your maximum heart rate would be 180. Your target zone for your walking heart rate should be between 60 per cent and 85 per cent of this maximum heart rate. For a 40-year-old person this would be between 108 and 153.

Take your pulse after you have been walking for about 5 minutes. If your heart is beating at a rate above your target zone then you are walking too vigorously. If you are unfit you would probably need to be walking at about 3 miles an hour to reach your target zone.

Table 1. Your Heart Rate Chart

Age	Maximum heart rate (Beats per minute) (220 minus your age)	Target zone	
		60%	85%
25	195	117	166
30	190	114	162
40	180	108	153
50	170	102	145
60	160	96	136
65+	155	93	132

A person in excellent physical condition could be walking at 4–5 miles an hour before reaching the target zone. Remember, though, you are not competing with anybody, not even with yourself, so start slowly. And if you cannot carry on a conversation whilst walking without gasping for breath you are going too fast.

How Fit Are You?

Few people have any real idea of how fit they are. Many men and women take a lot of exercise in the course of their daily activities yet consider themselves not very fit. Other men and women take a little regular exercise and think they are 'pretty fit'.

Clearly, fitness is relative to the purpose for which it is being achieved but there is also an acceptable level of general fitness which doctors describe as the capacity of the heart and muscles to use oxygen for energy production. To find out how fit you might be relative to other people try these tests.

Your Resting Heart Beat

This is a reliable and simple way of assessing your cardiovascular fitness. Take your pulse rate when you have been resting for some time or on first waking in the morning. Individual rates will vary, but you can use the Table to give yourself a fitness rating.

Table 2.   Your Resting Heart Beat

Age	20–29	30–39	40–49	50+
Men				
Excellent	59	63	65	67 or less
Good	60–69	64–71	66–73	68–75
Fair	70–85	72–85	74–89	76–89
Poor	86+	86+	90+	90+
Women				
Excellent	71	71	73	75 or less
Good	72–77	72–79	75–79	77–83
Fair	78–95	80–97	80–98	84–102
Poor	96+	98+	99+	103+

Your Physical Fitness

The step test is an excellent, research-proven way of testing your physical fitness, your aerobic fitness or cardio-vascular fitness. You can do the test yourself or with a partner.

1 Step onto a box or stair about eight inches high. Move one foot rhythmically after the other — left up, right up, left down, right down.

2 Keep to a pace of 24 complete step-ups a minute.

3 Do this for 3 minutes without stopping.

4 After 3 minutes stop. Sit down. After 30 seconds of rest take your pulse. Count the number of beats for this 30-second period. Multiply this figure by two. This is your heart recovery rate score.

5 Consult the Table to find your fitness grade.

Table 3. Your Fitness Grade

Age	20–29	30–39	40–49	50+
Men				
Excellent	74	78	80	83
Good	76–84	80–86	82–88	84–90
Fair	86–100	88–100	90–104	92–104
Poor	102+	102+	106+	106+
Women				
Excellent	86	86	88	90
Good	88–92	88–94	90–94	92–98
Fair	99–110	95–112	96–114	100–116
Poor	112+	114+	114+	118+

4

Walking Your Weight Away

'Weight problems can result from compulsive eating caused by emotional stress. Walking can alleviate such stress.'

Medical Editors, 'Walkways' Washington DC

Try solving this little problem. Sarah and Sally Craig are twins, each weighing 130 pounds. They work in the city; Sarah is an insurance assessor, Sally is in banking. The only exercise they get between 9 o'clock and 5 o'clock each day is an occasional walk from one office to another and down to the staff canteen. Both are health and figure conscious; each chooses her meals carefully.

Sarah goes out jogging on Monday, Wednesday and Friday evening, covering a mile in 10 minutes. She returns perspiring freely, has a shower and then listens to music or goes out in her car to visit friends.

Sally does no exercise at all when she gets home in the evenings and spends most of her time playing the flute or painting. However, she does walk the mile to the station each morning in just over 15 minutes and the same mile on the homeward journey.

The question is: which of the women burns the most calories in a week? To help you with your calculations you can use the following information based on medically tested facts (from US President's Council on Physical Fitness and Sport): a 10-minute one-mile job burns 25 more calories than a 15-minute one-mile walk for a person weighing 130 pounds. Thus in one week, Sarah jogs 3 miles, Sally walks 10. Do you need a calculator to work out that Sally, without sweat, is walking her weight away more effectively than Sarah? No? It is obvious she is. Walking is the key to weight loss and weight control.

Work it out this way, says psychologist Martin Katahn, Director of the Weight Management programme of Vanderbilt University. 'A brisk 45-minute walk will burn up 200 calories. Just expending that 200 calories a day would mean 20 or 30 fewer pounds of fat a year.' In two years those who are grossly overweight would be 4 stones lighter!' The slim lean look for a mere 200 calories' worth of walking a day. (See chart on p. 44.)

Just by walking?

Well, not exactly. You would also have to watch what you ate. Consider the experience of the woman walker mentioned in the Guinness Book of Records, Helen Krasner. After her 5,000 mile walk around the coastline of Britain, in hot sunshine and freezing rain, she weighed herself.

'Had you lost a stone or two in weight?' I asked. The answer was surprising.

'I had put on 20 pounds and had to go on a slimming diet!'

They say it's the exception that proves the rule. But how could anyone walking 17 miles a day for 10 months gain so much weight? Helen explained: 'I was nibbling food all day. Perhaps to pass the time, perhaps because I thought it would replenish my energy stocks, perhaps through boredom. And then at the end of each day I would sit down to a good hot meal.'

We can all learn something from Helen's experience. Nibbling when you feel like food is sometimes recommended as a means of losing weight — the small, but often method. But you can't have it both ways. If you're going to nibble you must not sit down to regular meals as well. In any case, think how difficult it is to measure just what your calorie intake is when you are always nibbling.

How Do You Eat?

Let's be realistic. We all have our own particular eating style: nibbling, bulk-eating, sweet-munching, fast-feeding, and so on. Some of us may have a mixture of styles, but we can still adapt our ways of eating to cater for our own particular needs.

All you have to do is to take time to plan your eating programme so that it does not detract from the beneficial effects of your walking routine. If you are a nibbler, then work out a time-table and menu for your frequent small meals: breakfast, mid-morning break, lunch, mid-afternoon break, tea and supper time. Have your small snacks made up for work and non-fattening food in the fridge for when you eat at home.

The bulk-eater who likes to feel satisfyingly full after a meal can still achieve this sense of satisfaction from big helpings of salad and fresh vegetables. People who like sweet foods can use fresh fruit as dessert or as a natural sweetener. The muncher must avoid peanuts and crisps and satisfy the desire to chew with crunchy apples, carrots and similar foods.

Fast-eaters hardly know what they have eaten. Food for them disappears like fluff down a vacuum cleaner leaving little sense of having had a meal. Fast-eaters must slow down if they are not to eat more calories than they are expending in walking energy fuel. Try the following little dodges:

- savour the taste of each mouthful;
- take smaller bites;
- chew food longer;
- use your napkin more often;
- sip a glass of water occasionally;
- pause to talk or read;
- above all tell family and friends not to push second helpings on you.

Walking to Your Ideal Weight

Think carefully about your diet so that you can now walk to your ideal weight, and maintain it. Study a calorie content list and have fun preparing meals that come well within your planned calorie intake. Finally one more piece of advice which goes against everything parents used to drill into children. It's advice that comes straight from the Weight Watchers' Handbook: 'Resign from the clean plate club!'

Not-so-tasty morsels can be left. Carry a mental picture of the surplus food mountain you are creating by letting some always go into the bin in the kitchen.

When you think about diet in this way your energy input will be lower than your energy output. This is the only way to lose weight and keep slim. The gap between input and output is one that the urban walker can easily widen, without much hardship or need for stoic willpower.

For those who like scientific statistics, physiologists say

that approximately 3,500 calories taken surplus to energy requirements would be stored as a pound of fat. So, if 100 calories are not used as energy fuel each day for 35 days, then your body will have an extra one pound of fat to carry about as you walk.

The equation of input and output works cumulatively. If you eat an extra slice of bread (1½ ounces) each day above your energy requirements this could lead to about 10 pounds of fat creeping on to your body frame in a year. Correspondingly, to lose 10 pounds a year, you only need to create a yearly energy deficit of 35,000 calories or 100 calories a day.

Tipping the Balance

You can tip the balance between calorie input and output so that it works favourably for you by:

- increasing energy expenditure — walk more than you used to do;
- eating less, leave food on your plate, not your waistline.

Val Hobbs, a secondary school teacher, was making the evening meal for her husband when she suddenly became aware, yet again, that her clothes were too tight for her. She placed the casserole of braising steak on the table with a certain touch of finality and said: 'That's it. I'm sorry I can't eat it with you. I'm far too fat. I can't sit and watch you eat either, so I'm going out for a walk.'

That was 6 months ago when she weighed a ridiculous 14½ stones. She joined a slimming club and reduced her daily energy intake to 1,200 calories to give her an estimated deficit of 1,000 calories each day (7,000 a week, or 28,000 a month). The pounds dropped away. But she wanted to lose weight even faster so she deliberately walked more at school, forcing herself to battle through corridors crowded with pupils pushing and shoving; she walked upstairs when she had no real need, marched into the town shopping centre each lunchtime whether she had anything to buy or not, and she walked to work and back every day.

The pounds slipped off even faster and when she told her colleagues about her walking one of them said: 'I'm shattered enough already each day. I'd never manage with all that walking as well.'

It was the sort of thing many people would say now. But

Val Hobbs disillusioned them: 'The funny thing was that I too thought I'd be too tired to work with all the extra walking, but strangely enough I seemed to have plenty of energy. I felt better for it very quickly.'

Sometimes we forget how much people used to walk before there were as many cars, buses and trains around. Yet if we look a little way back in history we can find countless examples of how much walking people used to do on top of a strenuous day's work.

Tom Richardson, a 6-foot one-time England fast bowler, weighed 12 stones at the peak of his fitness and regularly walked the 6 or 7 miles from his home near Mitcham to the Oval cricket ground with his heavy cricket bag on his shoulder. No other fast bowler had ever produced remotely comparable figures to those he achieved in his prime.

The legendary Wilfred Rhodes, also a professional cricketer for England and Yorkshire, enjoyed the publicity and prestige of a Prime Minister yet he walked miles to work. In those days he would return from a Yorkshire match in the South of England early in the morning, walk up the hill from Leeds station to Kirkheaton carrying his bag containing four or five bats, pads, boots, blazer, in one hand and a suitcase in the other. Later in the morning he would walk back to the station again and be on the field, fit and fresh at 11 o'clock.

My grandfather Bob Stout, a Penrith farmer, would drive his cattle into market at daybreak, a trip of 14 miles there and back down rough tracks, and then do a day's work afterwards. Today cattle go to market by truck and farmers ride about the fields on tractors. Men and women once expected to have to walk what we now consider to be long distances. Country children, and those in towns, would often have to walk 3 miles to school.

They took all this in their stride, and considered it nothing worth mentioning. You too can do just that. Do not underestimate your body's capabilities. Go out and walk, save yourself a lot of hassle and money as well. Be more independent of modern technology. Return to the old natural ways of travelling.

There was a time when people did not have to listen to advice given by government ministers telling them to get on their bike and find work. The 'tramping artisan' walked all over the country looking for work wherever he could find it. Their bodies were no different to ours except that they used them more and probably on less food. This is something we could all think about.

Waist Whittling

Oddly enough, though all the facts about dieting and exercise have been fairly common knowledge for a number of years, it is only recently that acceptance has been given to the waist-whittling effects of walking.

We have all seen the publicity given to the achievements of marathon runners, but how many of those viewers watching races on television would know that the winner of those gruelling 26-mile races would have used 1,000 *fewer* calories than an ordinary man or woman walking at a normal pace for 8 hours? You don't even have to walk continuously for 8 hours. You can build up your mileage total throughout the day or week.

Keep a record of your walking and your weight. Then you will avoid the twentieth century phenomenon — sometimes called 'creeping obesity' — whereby average men and women aged between 35 and 55 years thicken around the waist line and put on between 6 and 8 pounds every decade. And how dangerous this is need not be stressed: we know all too well how it can lead to heart attacks and high blood pressure.

Fortunately there is a simple way of whittling away this flab. Len Dawson found it. He is a 35-year-old joiner, and according to the charts showing the recommended daily calorie intake for the average man in certain trades, he needed 3,000 to do his job. If he expends that 3,000 calories each day, then his weight remains the same. But if he takes more exercise on top of this then he will lose weight. Body tissues are burned as energy fuel. And this is just what he did to reduce his weight to that recommended by his doctor. He walked more every day.

It is the best long-term solution to weight control — walking more instead of tackling a rigorous slimming diet. By adding 200 calories' worth of exercise a day — two 20-minute sessions of brisk walking to and from work — you could lose weight without having to modify your diet very much.

As an approximate guide to the calories used in walking by men and women of different body weights consult the chart below. From this you can work out what your own require-ments will be.

Table 4.   Calories Burnt in Walking for an Hour

Speed of walking mph	Weight in pounds						
	100	120	140	160	180	200	220
2	130	160	185	210	240	265	290
2½	155	185	220	250	280	310	345
3	180	215	250	285	325	360	395
3½	205	248	290	330	375	415	455
4	235	280	325	375	420	470	515
4½	310	370	435	495	550	620	680

Charles Whitmore used the figures on a chart like the one above to work out his walking schedule after his doctor had given him the shock of his life. Charles was what people might call a 'fine figure of a man', but just a little gone to seed. He had been an athlete in his younger days, but had not had much time for sport since joining a public relations firm in the city. He had done well and had been instrumental in signing up many good new accounts; he was a hard-working personable sort of chap who had an eye for detail. It was this aspect of his character which moved him to go for a medical check although he was feeling no real symptoms of stress or illness. He knew he had an expanding waist line, but thought that was just something one acquired in one's thirties.

The doctor told him straight. 'Your blood pressure is dangerously high. You're heading for a stroke or heart attack. I can put you on pills to reduce the blood pressure, but I think it would be better if you could get to grips with the problem yourself and see how it reacted to loss of weight and a bit of regular exercise. Come and see me again in about a month: or before, if you have any feelings of ill health.'

The next day Charles Whitmore deliberately did not go to work. Instead he went out for a long leisurely walk and thought things through in his usual careful manner, as he would have done a problem at work. He had read all the health education pamphlets the doctor had given him, and by the time he had walked until lunchtime he had come up with the right answer. It was, of course, a simple one of exercising more and eating less. His weekly target was a modest and achievable one of having a 3,500 calorie deficit, through exercise and diet. He had done his calculations carefully. He was very much surprised therefore by the weight he registered on the doctor's scales a month later. It was far lower than his calculations had led him to expect. He was not a man to keep his bewilderment to himself and asked the doctor how it was that he had lost so much more weight than he had expected.

The doctor explained to him that the physical exercise of walking has an effect upon the body's metabolism in addition to that of burning extra calories as energy fuel. During walking, when the heart and respiratory rate increase, the metabolic processes also speed up, and it takes some time after the exercise has finished for them to slow down to a more normal rate. The phenomenon can be compared to a fire being wafted into a fierce blaze and continuing to burn brightly for some time afterwards.

Charles Whitmore was soon enjoying all the other extra bonuses that come with exercise walking. The reason why is explained in the US Surgeon General's Report on Health and Disease Prevention as follows:

People who exercise regularly report that they feel better, have more energy, often require less sleep. Regular exercisers often lose excess weight as well as improve muscular strength and flexibility. Many also experience psychological benefits including enhanced self-esteem, greater self-reliance, decreased anxiety, and relief from mild depression.

Moreover, many adopt a more healthy life style — abandoning smoking, excessive drinking, and poor nutritional habits.

Sustained exercise improves the efficiency of the heart and increases the amount of oxygen the body can process in a given period of time. Compared to non-exercisers, people who engage in regular physical activity have been observed to have a one and a half to two times lower risk of developing cardio-vascular disease, and an even lower risk of sudden death.

Charles Whitmore achieved his goal with no trouble at all. What about you?

Your Goal Weight

Can you still get into the clothes you wore a few years ago? Is the waist-band too tight? Will the skirt zip fasten easily? The size and fit of your clothes gives an immediate hint of what is happening to your figure and weight. But is this adequate? It is not. You need the following:

- bathroom scales,
- an accurate assessment of what you should weigh (see chart on p.49)
- a record book.

A good guide to the ideal weight for a healthy person expecting a long life would be the one worked out by the American Insurance companies who carefully assessed all their combined data on 5 million clients over a 10-year period. For each height they worked out the weights which went with those men and women who lived the longest. Furthermore, these weights were then adjusted to allow for individual variations in body frame and type.

It is not always easy to say accurately which particular body type you are, and so the reaslistic way of deciding what your own ideal weight should be according to the tables is to make sure that it falls within the broad range given. If you are outside this range of suitable weight then you need to watch your diet and take more exercise.

Now look at the chart and decide which body weight you should have as your goal.

Your Own Walking Programme

If you no longer have that trim youthful waistline; if it is looking middle aged, then here is great news for you. There is a swift and simple way of getting into a healthier and more attractive shape: your own 'weight away' walking campaign.

Daily routine

Walk briskly — aerobically — for at least 20 minutes every other day and walk just as far at a leisurely pace on alternate days. Aim to increase your daily mileage by 3 to 4 miles. You can do this by adding a little extra walking here and there during the course of the day. Remember there is a bonus here too in that the metabolic rate speeds up when you walk and continues at a higher than normal rate when you sit down again. Keep giving it cause for pepping up.

Weekly schedule

The cumulative effect of an extra few miles each day could add a surprising 15 or 20 miles each week. At weekends, find excuses and reasons for walking more: park your car further away from shopping and entertainment centres; go for a family hike in the country, or on the quiet urban streets.

One energetic urban walker friend has designed a series of treasure hunts which his children look forward to doing with him on Sundays in the city whilst his wife goes swimming. During the week he spends his lunch hour walk searching for interesting landmarks, decorative figures, even unusual postboxes. He lists them in order along a route which his children have then to find and follow. Consequently on Sundays he and his children are walking excitedly together looking for the next clue and not thinking at all about exercise.

Weekend walking can help you to make up for any shortfall in mileage which you might inadvertently have incurred during the week.

Monthly goals

An opportunity for the urban walker to see just how much progress has been made in the quest for physical fitness is provided by tackling a long walk once a month. In this way you will have positive evidence that you are indeed becoming stronger and fitter. You will be walking further and with less effort. This is the time you will feel like congratulating yourself on your achievements.

And the categorical proof of your energy output will be staring you in the face — on the face — of the bathroom scales. Pounds lighter! Isn't it all worthwhile?

Will Walking Increase Your Appetite?

The indolent cynics can often be heard to say that walking is a self-defeating activity for slimmers because the exercise stimulates the appetite and you eat more. This might lead to a weight increase through eating more calories than are expended in the course of the physical activity. This argument has no scientific validity.

Both experience and research suggest that walking and other forms of exercise can curb the appetite. Taking vigorous exercise does not necessarily mean that you will want to eat a bigger meal afterwards. What in fact happens is that the more physically active you are, the more is your appetite reflexively adjusted so that you take in no more food than you need. Walking can actually subdue your appetite.

It was with this in mind that Jean Niditch, who founded Weight Watchers, advised her clients to take a walk whenever they felt a craving for food. The idea is supported by Laurence Morehouse, Professor of Exercise Physiology at the University of Los Angeles, who writes: 'Physical inactivity leads to increased food intake. Cattle raisers know this and pen their stock. The result of inactivity is a rapid gain of body fat and softening of muscle tissue.'

Do not let the cynics put you off with their fallacious ideas about increased eating after physical activity. Walking is an ideal way of combining 'caloric burn' with dietary restraint, so it is easy to walk your way to a 500-calorie deficit a day without upsetting your metabolism or your appetite, and without feeling either strain or starvation. It is the most simple way of achieving a debit balance of 3,500 calories a week and thus losing a pound of fat.

Effective Weight Control

Losing weight is only the beginning of the ongoing process of effective weight control. People achieve their goal weight in a sustained burst of enthusiasm and then, if they are not careful, the tide rolls in, the inches and pounds creep back, taking them unawares, and before they quite realise what has happened they are back with their tight waist-bands and flabby hips.

But not the urban walker.

Habits of walking by this time will be ingrained and will have become part of the normal day's routine. By this time no-one is willingly going to lose all the gains from walking by returning to over-eating. Whilst those relying entirely on a restricted diet are almost always doomed to failure, the walker will achieve a stable weight, for he or she will know just how to make adjustments in walking routines to get rid of any surplus weight just as soon as it appears on the record sheet.

Ideal Height/Weight

Height ft in		Men			Women	
	Small Frame st lb	Medium Frame st lb	Large Frame st lb	Small Frame st lb	Medium Frame st lb	Large Frame st lb
4 8	—	—	—	6 11	7 3	7 13
4 9	—	—	—	6 13	7 6	8 2
4 10	—	—	—	7 1	7 9	8 5
4 11	—	—	—	7 5	7 12	8 8
5 0	—	—	—	7 8	8 1	8 11
5 1	8 5	8 11	9 7	7 11	8 4	9 0
5 2	8 7	9 1	9 10	8 0	8 7	9 3
5 3	8 10	9 4	10 0	8 3	8 11	9 7
5 4	8 13	9 7	10 2	8 6	9 1	9 11
5 5	9 2	9 10	10 7	8 10	9 5	10 1
5 6	9 6	10 0	10 12	9 0	9 9	10 5
5 7	9 11	10 4	11 2	9 4	9 13	10 9
5 8	10 0	10 9	11 7	9 9	10 3	10 13
5 9	10 5	10 13	11 10	9 13	10 7	11 3
5 10	10 9	11 3	12 1	10 3	10 11	11 8
5 11	10 13	11 8	12 6	10 7	11 1	11 12
6 0	11 3	11 12	12 10	10 11	11 5	12 2
6 1	11 7	12 3	13 1	—	—	—
6 2	11 11	12 8	13 6	—	—	—
6 3	12 1	12 13	13 11	—	—	—
6 4	12 5	13 4	14 2	—	—	—

Although dieters may lose some fat by abstaining from fattening foods they also lose some lean body tissue, but the walkers who watch their diet not only lose fat, but also gain lean muscular tissue which makes them feel better and look younger.

There is another aspect of effective weight control we have not yet mentioned. This is the cause of over-eating: there may be many. Psychologists explain over-eating as a form of solace to those who feel insecure. Children of broken homes, those who feel unwanted and those who fear the loss of their partner's love, often over-eat to compensate for emotional insecurity or frustration. For them, food symbolises security. Excess pounds might result from this form of psychological craving or they may just be the cumulative effect of wrong eating habits over many years.

There is also another reason that causes people to eat too much: it is stress. It has been found that some people under stress in their working or home situations, or under the threat of uncertainty due to redundancy or having to move home, often eat more than they would when settled in a serene way of life. Extra eating during short-term stress can lead to long-term bad eating habits. Learning to cope with stress can help to break this pattern.

Here again walking can be a great help. A walk can be as good for your mind as it is for your body. It can go a long way towards removing stress which is a condition that has the potential for producing really harmful changes in the body chemistry and structure, including obesity.

5

Walking From Stress To Serenity

'A vigorous walk can be more effective than 400 milligrams of tranquilliser.'

Dr Herbert De Vries, Director of the Exercise Laboratory, University of California

The next time you drive to your bank's cash dispenser point and step out of your car to walk the 10 paces to the illuminated box on the wall, pause for a moment, compose yourself and resolve not to become irrationally angry if you find behind the transparent shield, a small notice saying 'closed'. Keep calm. Or you could be about to kill yourself.

The Cash Point Killer

A specialist in stress-induced illness, Dr Terry Looker, of Manchester Polytechnic, has just produced a new warning for all users of automated devices. He says that poorly functioning public utilities can cause heart attacks and early death. He maintains that even the humble cash dispenser, though a source of infinite joy to many, can be a potential killer, when, as often happens, the insertion of the card brings the mournful message: 'out of order'.

Amidst a whole range of potential 'death traps', Dr Looker drew attention to those long cordoned queues in post offices leading to poker-faced clerks which cause such rage and frustration, that all over Britain, it seems, 'victims' are being whisked away to an early grave.

Other sources of stress-related apoplexy identified by doctors are: switching to new technology, getting things repaired while at work and coping with bureaucracy.

Teachers, doctors, and nurses who feel thwarted by the constraints under which they work are at a particularly high risk. As many as one in thirty doctors eventually die by their own hand.

At a conference of top stress-management experts, Dr Keith Thanatoulos of the Health Hazard Research Institute put forward another cause of stress-related death encountered these days which he said was reading articles warning of new, hitherto undreamed of health hazards!

When people read headlines such as 'Cash dispensers can kill', particularly if they have read seven other articles that same week warning them that the public is at risk from drinking milk or chewing Taiwanese Christmas decorations, they can easily keel over from shock or boredom or both.'

Let us then put stress in its right perspective. The easiest way, of course, is to put the scare-mongering papers down and just go for a walk, the traditional Anglo-Saxon cure for stress. But instead we will take a short, but serious look at what stress really is.

Meeting the Demands of Stress

Stress is there whether we like it or not. We all respond in some way or other to the environment, to the things and people around us. Think, for example, how you react to being held up in a queue at one of the British Rail travel information offices whilst an elderly person twitters on about possible alternative routes of travelling while your own train is just about to leave or arrive. Do you get hot under the collar? Do you feel angry that only three of the six information assistant's places are occupied? Do you feel like asking to see the manager? If you do you are not alone. Thousands of people are reacting to situations like this every day. And within your body there will be a complex interaction of systems taking place. The frustration is not just in your head. It is seeping through your whole body. It could be making you ill.

The body's reaction to too much stress is one of 'fight or flight', which manifests itself as palpitations, heart throbbing and feelings of weakness. This may lead to mental breakdown, high blood pressure or chronic low-back pain, sometimes a euphemism for mental pain. It is important therefore that we understand the causes of stress and how to deal with them.

Today, for young and old alike, life is full of stresses — there is no limit to those situations which put pressure on us, frustrate, irritate or make us boil with suppressed rage. Compared with our parents and grandparents we live at a much faster pace and have higher expectations as we rush from one set of circumstances to another.

What can we do when faced with incompetence, indifference and malfunctioning devices? Over and over again we have the option of verbally abusing some innocent employee who can give us little comfort, or of consuming ourselves in the fire of our own helpless anger. But what happens when we do protest to management at the highest level? Often we receive little satisfaction. A man was so irritated with his 'ultimate driving machine' that he wrote to the ultimate boss. The reply he got was reported to have been: 'Tough!' It takes little imagination to envisage what that one word did for the writer's blood pressure.

A woman who complained to the Chief Executive Officer of her local council about the newly erected and enormously expensive public toilets being locked at 3 o'clock in the afternoon was received with stoic resignation by a man who could only shrug his shoulders and mutter, 'Vandals.' He might just as well have lifted his eyes to heaven and said: 'It is the will of Allah!'

If one is frustrated what can one do? There must be a way of dealing with these twentieth century irritations. Some people cope by lowering their expectations or by adopting Job-like patience. But if we all followed that example we should soon find ourselves living in a worse mess than ever. There are times when we have to protest in the interest of fair play and of maintaining standards. The well-known letter writers — 'Indignant of Easingwold' and 'Irritated of Tunbridge Wells' have done much in their day for us all. But what have they done for their own health? What should we do when we feel angry and powerless? One excellent way of defusing such a situation is to go out for a walk, to get some fresh air and see things in their right perspective. There is nothing to be gained from retreating to your own room to stick pins in wax effigies, nor is there any satisfaction to be achieved from telephoning indifferent bureaucrats in the middle of the night just to get your own back.

Avoiding the Props

Stress causes more misery, illness and death than many of the more feared diseases of today, and until recently the most likely remedy to be prescribed was anti-depressant and tranquillising drugs. Taking tablets is not always a bad thing. The prescription of a particular drug to help you over a major crisis can be one of the most useful steps a doctor can take for you, but what you should remember is that medication does not help to resolve the underlying problem. It cures only the symptoms of anxiety. Furthermore, drugs can diminish your ability to tackle problems effectively. Your doctor will advise you how to withdraw from tranquillisers.

Your aim should be to avoid the props if you can — and these include tobacco and alcohol. When you're bubbling with suppressed anger or anxiety there's a temptation to reach for a cigarette to ease the stress of the moment. Women, it seems, are now more likely to be doing this than men. Statistics show that while the number of men who smoke is decreasing, the number of women smokers is not. Such is the pressure on the working woman these days — 11 million women in Britain make up 42 per cent of the workforce, and many of those in positions of responsibility are smoking more. Women who averaged 87 cigarettes a week in 1972 now get through 96. In the short term tobacco might give some relief, but at what cost? A breath of fresh air and a short stroll through the streets can be far more relaxing and revitalising.

The short-term use of drugs had proved even more disastrous. Forty three year old Sheila Moorhouse was prescribed Ativan 12 years ago for the stress disorders she was suffering as a teacher in a tough Liverpool comprehensive school. Her doctor assured her that the drug was harmless and she continued taking the tablets even after the traumatic term had passed, for she found life was more bearable that way. And so she continued for the next eight years, but during this time she was developing a tolerance for the tranquillising drug and needed increasingly larger doses. Eventually she sank into the blackest depression which neither Ativan nor anti-depressant drugs could alleviate.

She became so ill and desperate that she agreed to go into a hospital drug dependence unit for six weeks. There she weathered the horrific withdrawal symptoms.

I was overcome with the most tremendous fear which was like constant panic. I was terrified of everything and everybody and it was as if I had landed in a threatening world. I suffered insomnia for six months at the same time as being hyperactive. I became an exhausted body dragged around by my own tireless adrenalin. I had pain in one side of my neck and a numbness on the left side of my face.

But she at last recovered. She had learnt the hard way, though, that short-term props can become long-term problems.

Sometimes we can take effective action to solve difficulties by thinking them through on a long walk. Or by going on a long walk to give the mind a complete rest from the problems: literally walking away from the problems. Walking can give us a physiological boost as well as a psychological one; we feel better and therefore get a lift in our spirits.

Preparing for a Stressful Day

Sometimes a quiet walk each morning can do much towards identifying the underlying causes of stress and enable you to seek out new and safe ways of relieving the conditions causing worry or pressure. It is interesting, for example, to see how some world leaders use the morning walk to prepare themselves for a stressful day's diplomacy.

The point is very well illustrated by what happened at one of the most critical of European conferences of recent times — an emergency Common Market summit meeting aimed at averting the bankruptcy of the European Community. British Prime Minister Margaret Thatcher, looking grim-faced and resolute, arrived in her Daimler Jaguar; West German Chancellor Kohl emerged from a long-wheel-based Mercedes resolutely determined to defend his politically powerful small farmers. Other premiers followed, equally lugubrious. Clearly no one was going to relish the battle between the giants, the clash of wills over agricultural reforms aimed at resolving the Community's chronic financial crisis. For everyone at that meeting, a gloomy day of tension, flagging spirits and mounting stress lay ahead.

But one of the 'giants' had not yet arrived. Where was he? At last he appeared, looking as laid-back as ever, hat in hand, followed by a phalanx of scurrying security men, walking briskly through the streets of Brussels. Seventy one year old President Mittérand of France was getting himself in a relaxed frame of mind for the taxing day before him. He knew that the meeting would be an acrimonious one. But he surely did not expect tempers to rise to such a pitch that his French Prime Minister, Jacques Chirac — admittedly a man known for his occasional indelicacy of language — would jump to his feet in sheer frustration and utter an enormous obscenity, 'Couillons!' (Bollocks!)

Tension in the chamber mounted dangerously. The Chairman, Chancellor Kohl of West Germany, asked M Chirac to withdraw the remark, others fumed with indignation.

And the cool M Mittérand? What did he do? He went out for a walk. His recipe for dealing with stress was to take some fresh air striding round the magnificent medieval Grand Place.

Walking can defuse not only situations, but also the highly sensitive explosive we all have within our bodies. Each time some of that goes off, the body most likely to be harmed is our own.

Walking Away from Stress

We all have to cope with stressful situations, Sometimes we can literally walk away from them, going in a different direction and actually avoiding a confrontation, which is what Dr John Hunter advised people (and himself) to do. In tragically prophetic words he once said: 'My life is in the hands of any rascal who chooses to annoy me.' He had been suffering from cardiac pain and knew very well that his salvation lay in walking away from stressful arguments and similar situations. Unfortunately there was one occasion when he could not walk away to protect his peace of mind. After a frenetic committee meeting at St George's hospital he died from a heart attack.

Walking can be a life saver.

Yorkshireman George Garbutt is a great advocate of this kind of stress therapy. He is one of the few headmasters of a state comprehensive school who managed to soldier on right up to his retirement at the age of 65. He is a delightful man with a wealth of experience and a fund of anecdotes, a teacher par-excellence and a lover of children. On the day when he had handed over his tough Doncaster school to the newly appointed head, he stood with his hand on the door-knob of his study to have a final look round and gave one last piece of advice.

There will be times, when so many problems appear on your desk you'll not know which to tackle first. It was on days like this that I'd leave my office and say to my secretary, Mrs Wilson, that I was off out for a 'liaison' visit. I'd walk out for half an hour and by the time I got back many of the problems had been solved — by themselves or other people — and I'd be ready to tackle the rest. Don't forget young man; take a walk, it'll do you a power of good.

And with that he walked out to a long retirement which he is still enjoying.

The great bonus of urban walking done at various times of the day is that it can counteract the harmful effects of cumulative stress. A walk can wipe the slate clean for the rest of the day. Continuous and excessive stress is not only bad for your health, it is also ageing. Tensed muscles remain cramped, blood pressure is pushed up higher and higher as each flash of anger or frustration adds to the toll until one day the body says, 'enough is enough,' and falls sick. Psychosomatic sickness it might be called, but the symptoms are real enough.

We can avoid the cumulative effect of stress by walking to give the mind a refreshing break. And we can give ourselves the stamina to deal with stress by walking too.

A trade union leader had a problem. He found that towards the end of a day's hard negotiating with industrial tycoons he was absolutely exhausted. And that was when he usually lost his bargaining power. In desperation he went to see a friend, a fitness expert who advised him to take up walking and tell everybody that lunchtimes would, from then on, always find him walking. Alone.

Months later the union negotiator told his friend: 'It was all so simple. Now I've got stamina to keep to a tough line longer than they have.'

You Are in Charge

Of course, there are bosses who tend to scoff at all talk of stress and pass it off as a new-fangled excuse for the faint-hearted. But that is not surprising, says Dr John Bonn, Director of the Stress Research and Management Unit at St Bartholomew's Hospital, London. Bosses, he says, are the people least likely to suffer from stress since they can pass all the problems down the line. It is the middle managers who suffer most.

What people have to remember is that no-one is managing your life for you and saying 'you must save time for exercise', or 'you must take 10 minutes off for a refreshing walk'. We all have to decide for ourselves what we want to do with our time and energy. If the busy workday schedule does not include at least some things that you can enjoy and that are beneficial to health, then it is surely time to readjust your life-style.

You can start by walking more.

Some researchers claim that while one per cent of working days are lost because of strikes, four per cent of the absenteeism among men and five among women is caused by stress-related illnesses. Would it not be worthwhile for managers at all levels to consider the viability of breaks for a walk during the working day?

Is it such a revolutionary idea? Thirty years ago young Japanese girls working on transistor radios in a Tokyo plant stretched in unison to a series of exercises controlled by a foreman with a whistle. The exercises performed twice a day helped to prevent the girls from making mistakes from boredom or fatigue and also it helped them to avoid postural abnormalities caused by long periods of sitting crouched over their work-benches. Ten minutes away from the bench made economic sense. Ten minutes away from your desk walking in the city could also make economic sense.

The British Army has followed such a policy for as long as records have been kept. Soldiers have 10 minutes flat out on their backs every hour during a route march, and there has always been a break between periods of instruction. Rest allows recovery. Time off from work is not necessarily time lost. And if that time is used in walking to have a change of scene, or as a means of being on one's own for a brief spell, the benefit is all the more noticeable.

Time Off for a Walk

Forty three year old John Birt, Deputy Director General of the BBC, is married with two children and freely admits that life is not easy.

I am definitely under a lot of pressure, but so is anyone in a similar position. To take it you have to understand precisely what you are trying to do so that you may learn how to solve problems. Secondly, you have to leave space for solitude. The danger is working so hard you have no time to reflect. I am keen on walking and keeping one whole day free at the weekend.

Many people recommend walking alone, including the man who is perhaps the best known walker in Britain — Alfred Wainwright. For years he toiled away in the town hall treasurer's office of his native Blackburn with its dingy houses, shabby streets and huge factory walls that shut out the sun, but he always went for a walk during those long working days. At the weekend he was then ready for his escape into the English Lake District. How well he remembers those days!

'On a day when I didn't have to wear a collar and tie I was a boy again,' he says. 'If I was heading for the hills I would set forth singing — not audibly, Heaven forbid — just in my heart.'

Alfred Wainwright got such pleasure from observing and recording what he had seen when out walking that he began to chronicle his walks in guides that have sold millions of copies and been carried in millions of back packs. Yet not a penny of the money they have earned has gone into his own pocket, but has been invested in the formation of an animal welfare centre in his beloved Kendal.

Walking gave Wainwright greater riches than money could buy. It gave him an inner serenity, a happiness beyond all other wealth.

But you don't have to walk into the countryside to replace stress with serenity. Many famous people prefer walking in the town. The writer Charles Lamb, for example, always cast his vote for walking in the city rather than the countryside. 'For the streets, noises, and sins of London, the mountains of Keswick might go hang,' he said. The hurry scurry of town life had irresistible attractions for this confirmed urban walker, who wrote: 'Let them talk of lakes and mountains and romantic dales — all that fantastic stuff; give me a ramble by night in London. A mob of men is better than a flock of sheep, and a crowd of happy faces jostling into the playhouse at the hour of six is a more beautiful spectacle to man than the shepherd driving his silly sheep.'

But be it through town or country it is the actual walking that matters when it comes to relieving stress.

Talking and Walking

Neil Redfern, one of the new breed of stress counsellors who has to try to alleviate some of the causes and effects of stress, deals with people from all trades and professions.

It is not only company directors who suffer from stress these days. I have had firemen, nurses, teachers, mill-managers, actors, dentists and policemen referred to me. Many come after they have had to change jobs, houses and sometimes partners. Quite often the cure lies in two words: 'talking and walking'. Instead of talking across a table or room we talk as we walk. It's less formal, relaxing and invigorating at the same time. I'm a great believer in the walking therapy.

For those who think that a trip to a stress counsellor might look like an admission of inefficiency, Dr John Bonn of St Bartholomew's hospital has this to say: 'Suffering from stress is not a sign of character weakness. It is an indication merely that your own resources are being outstripped by what is being demanded of you.'

No longer is it taboo for those under pressure to seek help for stress. People in special need are those who suffer from post-traumatic stress disorder, a condition prevalent in survivors of war and the victims of terrorism, accidents and violent crime. If such a condition is allowed to go unresolved, or worse, if suppressed with anti-depressants of the suspected habit-forming benzodiazepine family (which includes Valium, Librium and Ativan), the symptoms may continue indefinitely.

Police Inspector Mike Holley explained how he had suffered from post-traumatic stress. One night a gang of youths full of beer and brandishing flick-knives were causing a disturbance in the centre of Leicester. He went to separate two who were brawling. It was then that another 17-year-old lad stabbed him with a stiletto knife.

Three months later he was back at work, but he was suffering from post-traumatic stress disorder. Wisely he sought help from consultant psychiatrist Ian Fussey who explained that it was quite natural for him to feel as he did. He said it was the same feeling that women get after a miscarriage. It comes also with the death of a spouse, divorce and separation. All such shattering experiences are likely to impair bodily and emotional health. If those feelings are not resolved early on then problems can intensify. Sufferers become locked in a cycle of anxiety and depression. Walking and talking is the centuries-old recipe for escaping from this prison of the emotions. Walking in conjunction with specialist counselling can help to heal the scars of stress and build up the confidence and courage needed for facing work and life again.

To sum up, people who lead stressful lives are now finding that the best route to relaxation is often through the rhythmic movements of walking which can help to undo the tensions of the day. Walking perks you up and helps you to combat threatening situations. And it has the undeniable merit of being founded not on faddy exercise regimes, but on down to earth common sense.

Walking to Serenity

Try this little trick the next time you go for a walk: fill your mind with thoughts of all the things that have given you pleasure in the past and of those you can look forward to in the future. And as you stride rhythmically along the road to work hum a happy tune as the background music to your happy thoughts.

This is the advice given by psychologists and psychiatrists who have made walking part of their anxiety therapy. Dr Richard Driscoll of Easter State Psychiatric Hospital in Knoxville, Tennessee, believes this prescription works wonders because the physical exertion stimulates all the body systems into a heightened physical state, and associated with these physical changes there is a feeling of excitement and ultimately of achievement. These positive feelings push away the negative feelings of anxiety. Once again we come back to the old medical doctrine that 'action absorbs anxiety'.

And what about the music?

It is one of the oldest known ways of stimulating those essential emotions which evoke a beneficial mental and physical response. Feet tap, heads nod, fingers move rhythmically to the beat. These are the simple, superficial manifestations of its influence, but there are deeper ones. Music penetrates right into the body and soul affecting the way we live and what we can do.

Remember how Saul's melancholy evaporated under the influence of David's harp? 'It is an effective antidote to all destructive passions — of anger, sorrow, worry and fear,' says Homer talking of the prophylactic power of music.

When this power of music is coupled with the physical rhythms of walking it is even more powerful. 'It is the sovereign remedy against despair and melancholy and will drive away the devil himself,' said Robert Burton in the seventeenth century.

Think how music while marching has stiffened the resolution of soldiers going into battle and built up their courage. A band playing brings renewed vigour to soldiers on the march. We know this from centuries of experience, but this knowledge is now backed up by recent research which shows that lively music stimulates the pulse rate; the efficiency of the circulatory system increases, and we feel better, fitter and even younger.

As you walk to work in the morning you can bestir yourself by singing, as the great Lakeland walker Wainwright did, or you could use a personal stereo cassette player to provide music that stimulates vital secretions to flow through your body, and chemical compounds that can lift flagging spirits and revitalise you, putting youthful energy into your step.

Music as you Walk

One of the benefits to be gained from music as you walk is that the rhythm of the music helps you to walk at a steady pace; one that will have the right aerobic effect for you. You can choose your own music or buy pre-recorded tapes made specially for walkers.

There is always the possibility, especially with urban walking, that as you go through the streets you forget about the walking and your mind wanders onto interesting things and the people you pass on the way. It is then that your pace can slow down and before you know it, the fitness benefits from the walk are being diminished. When you have music motivating your feet, you can let your mind wander at will and with merely peripheral concentration you will keep marching steadily along.

You might not be marching into battle like the Lacedaemonians being led into the fight by flutes, but there can be battles other than the bloody encounters of war. There are many ways in which we have to fight today and we can make use of the powerful force within our very souls which can be reached by music. Its appeal is primitive and influences all parts of the body, even the way we walk. As the Roman philosopher Seneca said over 1,000 years ago: 'The care of the soul is man's most important duty, because from the soul issue our thoughts, from the soul our words, from the soul our expressions and indeed our very gait.'

There is so much that walking to music can do for us, physically and emotionally, that we should make the best possible use of it in our walking.

Just as music was used in wartime to stimulate workers in armaments factories — 'music while you work' — so we can use music for its functional effect in our walking. Although there is much still to be discovered about the specific ways in which musical elements elicit emotional responses, most psychologists believe that the rhythm and tempo of music probably influence the emotions associated with them. Fast music suggests energetic activities coupled with feelings of exhilaration and well-being; a slow regular rhythm calls forth calm, dignity, solemn and leisurely activities and the emotions that accompany them.

Now you can make your own walking to music programme designed for the particular emotional response you want at any particular time of day or night.

If you want to walk from stress to serenity then think about the words of Chinese philosopher Lin Yutang as he explains what music can do for us:

Music is pure sentiment itself, dispensing entirely with the language of words with which alone the intellect can operate. Music can portray for us the sounds of cow-bells and fish-markets and the battle field; it can portray for us even the delicacy of flowers, the undulating motion of the waves or the sweet serenity of the moonlight.

For those who need more scientific evidence there are the words of the famous Harvard University physiologist, Cannon, who wrote that when emotions are aroused by music the endocrine glands release adrenalin and other hormones which have a benign effect upon the body and the mind.

It costs so little to expose ourselves to the rejuvenating and relaxing forces of music and walking. Why don't we do it more often?

Like now, for example.

6
What's Afoot?

Or madly squeeze a right-hand foot
Into a left-hand shoe.

Lewis Carroll, *Through the Looking Glass*

According to Britain's erstwhile satirical dramatist, George Bernard Shaw, German boots in the last century were all the same. The Germans had not thought it necessary to make the right boot any different from the left. If that were so, which I am inclined to doubt, then the German boot and shoe industry has come a long way since then.

There have been revolutionary changes in shoe design in the recent years of the jogging boom. The market forces have given a push to the designers, technicians and testers and as a result the shoes now available are lighter, more durable and better able to serve their purpose. They are so comfortable and give so much support that men and women are wearing their 'sports' shoes as casual wear and even for walking to work. They might not yet be acceptable for formal office wear but that day is not far hence.

Shops today carry a vast range of shoes of all shapes and sizes which will fit almost any kind of foot.

For the urban walker, who is covering more miles than he did formerly, careful shoe fitting is of the utmost importance. Of course, when you start your new routine of walking to and from work and perhaps walking during the day too, you could wear whatever comfortable shoes you have at the moment. In fact Dr Harry Hlavac, foot specialist and writer of *The Foot Book*, would advise you to do just that. He says: 'If you are walking comfortably in your shoes — no matter what the style — and not experiencing any blisters, irritation or pain or fatigue, stay with that shoe. There is no reason to change.'

But shoes which seem all right at the moment might not feel quite so comfortable after a week of walking part of the way to work and back every day. Consequently you might decide to buy a pair of shoes more suitable for the new routine.

You should be prepared to answer some awkward questions. As soon as you enter the shoe shop or department store you could find yourself faced with a young, keen sales-assistant without much experience of walking or of selling shoes, who will ask: 'What exactly do you want?'

Do you know the answer to this question?

To answer, 'a pair of walking shoes' is not enough. There is now an enormous choice of new walking-style shoes which include casual shoes, running or jogging shoes, genuine lightweight walking shoes and hiking boots. You will have to look hard and be discriminating in your method of selection.

To help you here is an idea of what to look for in the ideal urban walking shoe.

The Urban Walker's Shoe

Physical medicine specialist Dr Henry Clampton, who has been an enthusiastic urban walker for many years, drew up a list of points to look for in choosing a shoe.

- Look for good, durable, cushion-soles which will absorb some of the shock as the foot meets the ground. This is particularly important when walking will be mainly on paved sidewalks and streets. Adequate cushioning is the key to avoiding blisters and foot problems.
- Go for round or square-toed shoes so that your toes can move freely. Pressure through tightness causes pain and blisters.
- Make sure the shoe gives support at the sides as well as over the arch. The feet should not be able to slide from side to side.
- Feel the heel part of the shoe. The 'heel counter' should give firm lateral stability. The back and sides of the heel should feel well gripped, though not too tightly held when you walk in the shoe.
- Try flexing the shoe in your hands before trying it on. The shoe should bend easily at the ball of the foot. It it does not,

then you could find yourself troubled with pains up the back of the Achilles tendon. The sole should be stiff only at the shank towards the back of the instep.

- Check the height of the heel. There has been argument over this ever since Julius Caesar made his soldiers add half an inch onto the heels of their sandals. Medical specialists feel that a heel height of three to five eighths of an inch is best because such an elevation enables the calf muscles to work in a position of optimum mechanical advantage. If the heel is much higher, this could lead to an imbalance of work between the muscles of the lower leg and result in tendon strain.

- Take special care with your choice of material. Leather shoes allow the foot to 'breathe' better than they can with some synthetic materials. Leather also provides better protection against snow and rain. But leather shoes are usually heavier than other types. However, there are some good combinations of leather and nylon mesh fabrics which provide protection and yet do allow the foot to breathe.

Trying the Shoes on

This is always a difficult stage to decide between several shoes of the right type, but here are some tips which are passed on from experienced walkers:

- Try on both shoes. If one of your feet is bigger than the other or has some slight misalignment round the base joint of the big toe, then choose the larger size.
- Stand up in the shoes and walk round the shop. Take plenty of time.
- Make sure your heel does not lift inside the shoe when you walk.
- Compare the weight of the new shoe with the one you are currently wearing. Heavy shoes are more tiring on a long walk.
- Remember you will be wearing thicker socks and so ideally you should wear these when trying on the shoes. There is no need for the urban walker to wear a heavy hiking sock, but probably it is best to wear a thicker sock than the sort that would be worn with a more fashionable shoe.
- Feel the inside of the shoe. It should be smooth and free from rough seams which can cause blisters.

● Kick the toes on the floor. Are your toes cramped too tightly at the end of the shoe? Is the toe of the shoe reinforced enough to protect your toes?

Socks

Socks are almost as important as shoes for foot comfort. If you intend walking a long way, then two pairs of socks are recommended; a thin pair to prevent chafing, and a thicker, outer pair to cushion your feet, keep warm, and absorb sweat. The feet can sweat as much as a cupful of perspiration a day: if it is not absorbed into the sock, perspiration can make the foot itchy and cause a rash. Sweat can also eat into the fabric of the shoes causing the seams to become frayed and curled at the edges. The shoes will then become uncomfortable and may be the cause of corns and blisters.

Foot Care

Whilst the factors affecting your choice of shoe are still fresh in your mind, it is worth emphasising yet again the need for a good cushion sole that will protect your feet by absorbing the shock of impact with each step you take. No matter how good your shoes are, every single step sends shock waves surging through your body, putting stress on joints, tendons, muscles and ligaments.

Look at it this way. When you are standing at ease on both feet, each foot carries only half of your body weight, but as soon as you begin to walk or run the whole of your body weight plus a certain amount of extra weight through momentum is transferred alternately from one foot to the other. The amount of pressure thrown upon each foot by an adult man or woman has been computed to be about equivalent to the body weight plus 40 pounds. If you calculate the number of times that your feet hit the ground in the course of 1 mile you can soon see that your feet take a pretty hefty pounding.

The bearer of a good deal of this stress is the longitudinal arch which transfers the body weight from heel to toe. Holding this dome-shaped structure in place are the powerful muscles and ligaments which also help to give the foot spring and elasticity. Black Africans have excellent feet, their arches are exceptionally supple and strong, but people in the Western World appear to have lost this tensile strength. Their feet are far more susceptible to strain. The big toe joint is particularly vulnerable, especially in a shoe with a rigid sole, and the bones of the feet can be bruised when there is inadequate cushioning.

If you find, after buying your walking shoes, that you would like more cushioning then you can buy orthopaedic 'shock stoppers'. These are cushioning devices which can be slipped into your shoes. Athletes who find that they give their feet a terrible pounding in their particular events use these in-soles. Fatima Whitbread, the European Gold Medallist and world record holder for women's javelin events, finds them a great help in the prevention of sore feet.

Care of the feet is very important. We are continually dependent on them for support and locomotion. They serve us incessantly and, fortunately for many people, we only really think about them when they begin to ache. And ache they will at some time for most people.

'Almost 90 per cent of Americans have foot problems of one kind or another,' Say Drs Edith Schafer and Robert Nirschl. It is the same story in Britain.

'Most people are born with perfect feet but four out of five develop some foot trouble later in life,' write consultants for the British United Provident Association (BUPA).

If you do notice pain in your feet then seek advice from your medical practitioner rather than exacerbating the condition thinking that you can walk through the pain. In some cases this will be possible, but in others you might be making the condition worse.

The foot is an enormously complex structure made up of 26 bones — seven in the main part of the foot (the tarsus), five bones in the forefoot (called the metatarsals), and all the small bones of the toes. Together with the 107 ligaments and 19 muscles, these bones form a flexible structure which is able to meet the great strains put upon it.

Relieving Foot Pain

Sometimes, however, foot-strain does occur. If medical diagnosis reveals a condition of foot-strain, then relief can sometimes be obtained by first aid treatment. Ease the tense ligaments of the arch by slipping arch supports into the shoe under the instep. Further rehabilitation can be effected by exercises which restore mobility to the foot joints and strength to the supporting muscles.

Painful feet should be treated immediately; otherwise the bony structure of the foot begins to change. The instep becomes flat and the heel falls inwards, out of line with the lower leg. The extent to which the arch has flattened may be seen by examining a wet foot print on a dry board.

The navicular bone on the top of the foot becomes more prominent and the pain worsens. Because of these structural changes, it can become more difficult to find shoes that fit properly and comfortably, for pain is caused by pressure of the shoe on the prominent navicular bone.

Furthermore, if the front arch of the foot gives way then the weight of the body falls more heavily on the base of the second, third and fourth toes, which become inflamed and tender. As the foot becomes progressively flatter the pain becomes more severe. It is the final warning of stretched ligaments, displaced bones and unaccustomed pressure on the nerves serving the sole of the foot.

Sometimes one can see women (and men) who are suffering, walking on the outer border of one foot or both, for relief. If nothing is done to correct the misalignment the pain will gradually ease over the years as the bones bed down in their new positions and the nerves become less sensitive to unaccustomed pressure on them. But when pain ceases altogether the condition will become chronic and the foot will no longer be that tensile shock absorber and spring for graceful movement that it used to be. Foot flexibility is lost and an awkward gait is inevitable.

Remedial action can be taken as soon as messages of pain appear indicating that muscles and ligaments supporting the foot arches are being strained. Such strain can be reduced immediately by sitting more instead of standing for long periods — if this is possible. It is also important to make sure that your shoes are giving adequate support to your arches. If he or she feels it warranted your medical practitioner might recommend special exercises under the supervision of a trained physiotherapist.

Do seek medical advice before tackling any course of foot exercises, for the foot problems are too wide-ranging for general treatment. There is, nevertheless, one exercise which everyone should learn — one which can be of enormous value in maintaining the strength of the intrinsic muscles which support the feet and also in retaining foot flexibility.

It can be practised throughout the day without anyone knowing what you are doing. It is the foot-arching exercise which surpasses all others in preventive care of the feet.

The Foot-Arching Exercise

Sit with your feet flat on the floor. Now draw your toes towards the heel, but at the same time try to keep the toes straight and lying flat on the floor. It can be done only by arching the foot into a dome. Once you can do it while sitting, try it when you are standing as well. Try spreading and curling your toes alternately; flex and point the whole foot. Move your foot at the ankle in every possible direction, rotate it then turn the sole inward and outward. Walk barefoot about the house as often as possible and as long as there is no risk of injury.

You cannot overdo foot exercises and though you might not now be troubled with your feet, remember that foot-strain can hit you when you least expect it and at any age. It may come after a long period of confinement to bed through illness, or as a secondary effect of pregnancy, but it is less likely to trouble those who are physically fit and have prac-tised foot exercises.

Minor Problems

Everyone has his own ideas about how some of the minor problems can be best dealt with, and let us face the fact now that whatever activities we follow, and however much fun they provide there will be some problems. Most of these can be overcome quickly.

Robert Sweetgall, who has dedicated himself to spreading the message of fitness walking on his 11,600 mile, 50 state walk around the USA, places particular stress upon foot care when he talks to schools, civic clubs and groups of people in the town squares through which he passes. 'Give your feet air as well as creams and powders,' he says. He is not always a popular visitor to cafés and restaurants when he takes off his shoes and socks to let his feet breathe under the table. But if people object he leaves.

One of the myths of foot care to be dispelled right away, is that you can toughen your feet so much that you never get blisters. Many walkers try hardening soft skin with a little surgical spirit, but even men of the marine corps and SAS get blisters sometimes.

Blisters are the bane of every walker. They can be sheer agony if left unattended. If you want to continue walking in any comfort at all, it is essential you take action as soon as you feel discomfort on a tender spot. A small blister should be covered with moleskin or adhesive tape to prevent further damage. Large and very painful blisters should be treated with the utmost care. They can be punctured with a sterile needle — make sure it really is sterile by placing it in boiling water — and allow the fluid to drain out of the blister bubble. Do not cut away the skin, and be sure to keep it free from infection. When all the fluid has drained from the blister cover it with a dressing. Do not be tempted to apply ointment as blisters need to dry out. Do not cover the blister with a plaster, but with a gauze patch and tape the edges down.

When you have finished the day's walking remove the dressing and allow air to reach the blister. When it has healed up protect the damaged area with a plaster until the area is completely recovered.

Apart from the precaution of having well-fitting shoes and socks, what more can be done? Try using foot powder. This reduces friction and gives some protection against blisters.

Corns are caused by pressure, for example, from a seam on the inside of the shoe that is pressing continually on one spot on the edge of the toe. Go to a good chiropodist or podiatrist and take with you the shoes you wear everyday. If you have never had specialist help of this nature before, then you are in for a delightful surprise. The pain can be cured straightaway in 90 per cent of cases and if the fault is found to be in the shoe then the trouble need not recur if you change the shoes, or remove the pressure point within the shoe.

A word of warning here. Avoid bathroom surgery!

It might seem like a simple operation for you or your spouse to cut out a troublesome corn with a razor blade or scalpel, but it is all too easy to allow infection to enter the wound that has been cut too deeply. This could develop into a major problem. Cases have been known of toes having to be amputated as a result of such infection.

Always seek specialist help. It is well worth the money.

Callouses are areas of thick hard skin which form under the heel, and the ball of the foot, and along the edge of the big toes. They can be extremely painful when blisters form beneath them.

To prevent callouses becoming too thick you can soak your feet well in a bath of warm water and then rub the hardened skin with a pumice stone. Do not do this when there is pain. Seek help from your podiatrist.

Ingrowing toe-nails can become so painful that walking any distance becomes an ordeal. Sometimes the condition becomes even more serious when the nail grows into the flesh at the side of the toe. Once again, seek specialist help.

Thereafter never cut the toe-nails away at the sides. Cut them straight across.

Verrucas are infectious warts which can be picked up at a swimming pool and can be even more painful and incapacitating than corns. Special wart-removing preparations can be used with success, but if the condition persists then see your doctor and have the verruca cut out.

Bruised heels are not often suffered by walkers though they sometimes occur through coming down heavily and unexpectedly on the heel from a greater height than usual. This is more likely to happen at night. A torch is a good safety measure for night walking. You can see and be seen.

Once you have adopted an urban walking life-style your feet will move towards the centre of your attention. Examine them periodically for red spots and tenderness that could indicate the beginning of trouble. Give them the care they deserve.

Stay off your feet at the end of the day for a short period. Raise them above the level of your head for a spell and try a warm foot-bath as an extra bonus for them after a very hard day. Follow this by a few moments of foot massage. It can make more than just your feet feel better.

Foot Massage

The value of foot massage has been recognised in every culture of the world throughout history. It has tremendous therapeutic and psychological benefits for the urban walker.

Consider the principal objectives. The aim of the massage is to relax the mind and muscles so as to promote the flow of blood and lymph. But there are other worthwhile benefits. Many people who would certainly benefit from regular foot massage never try it because they feel it is only for disabled people or highly trained athletes, but the giving and the receiving of massage helps relaxation, gives reassurance and a feeling of well-being.

England's leading practitioner of 'zone therapy foot massage' is Joseph Corvo. He explained to me that this type of massage was used by the ancient Chinese to diagnose and cure sickness and afflictions unconnected with the feet. The practice is based on the belief that all glandular systems and organs of the body have nerve endings in the fingers, toes and feet. And the application of pressure at specific points can achieve wonderful results.

Zone therapists subscribe to the theory that illness is caused by an accumulation of crystalline products around the nerve endings. The sensitive fingers of zone therapists find such deposits, make a diagnosis accordingly, and then alleviate (if not cure) the condition by manipulation, massage and pressure. Joseph Corvo says that you can treat yourself with tremendous success.

What have you to lose?

Doctors who have prepared a guide on fitness and health say: 'Beyond convenience and economy, the value of learning massage yourself, and encouraging someone close to you to learn, is the understanding and well-being gained and comfort shared.'

To sum up then, care of the feet can ensure that your urban walking routine is never hampered by painful foot conditions. Now you can go out and walk with confidence. Give your body and mind a healthy boost with your 'feet power'.

7
Fortune Favours the Fleet of Foot

'In the city, power walks; taxis are for those who meet other men's schedules.'

American Maxim

Some say, fortune favours the brave; others may echo the cynical words of Ben Jonson, who 300 years ago wrote of Fortune that it favoured fools. But in the world of the young upscale, upwardly mobile professional people of today it seems that Fortune favours the fleet of foot.

Thirty four year old Irwin Kemp is a case in point. In more ways than one. He is head trader of one of the largest and most aggressive American broking houses (part of Chase Manhattan) on Wall Street. His clients expect him to provide high calibre, considered, and dispassionate advice. They want to hear of profit opportunities guaranteed against loss. They want riches without risks. And sometimes they want his blood. For example, when he recently bought a batch of securities which turned out to be much less valuable than anticipated, his clients raised a hue and cry. They wanted his head on the block. To say, then, that Irwin Kemp is under continual stress, working as he does in a world where volatile foreign exchange markets rarely come to a halt, would be a gross understatement. And it has certainly not been an easy year.

Heads have indeed rolled as firms cut back on their staff. In the wake of the October 1987 global stock market crash when hundreds of millions of dollars were being lost on stock markets around the world, as panic-stricken investors were dumping their shares at virtually give-away prices, Irwin Kemp kept calm.

His friends wondered how.

And when the worst was over and the market settled down to its new lower level, he emerged relatively unscathed. Whilst other firms were doing very little business, Irwin Kemp was in and out of the market, beavering away all the time. His colleagues envy Kemp's ability to thrive on the very uncertainties that drive others to distraction. In the midst of the market turmoil he trades quietly and firmly with hard-nosed brokers on the Tokyo market at all hours of the day and night.

How does he manage to work at such a fast pace and for such long hours without cracking?

No one sees him drive into the senior executives' car park in the morning. He is always in his office by seven o'clock. No one sees him drive away in the evening. Which is not surprising, for Irwin Kemp leaves the building through a delivery door at the back. On foot.

He walks to work.

Early each morning, Irwin Kemp, immaculately dressed in his dark-grey, Brooks Brothers' suit, his striped, Brooks Brothers' button-down Oxford-cloth shirt, and with light-weight comfortable shoes and faithful Filofax in hand, he is picked up and driven part of the way to work by a neighbour — a retired army major who supplements his pension in a variety of ways. One of these is in driving Irwin Kemp and another is by modest investments on the stock market. That, in itself, is worth getting up early for.

Three or four miles away from his office, depending upon the weather and work commitments, Irwin Kemp leaves his limousine and sets off at a brisk pace, truly fleet of foot. He enjoys that period of exercise walking and the comparative peace of mind which it induces.

Once in his office he reads all the papers, checks the overnight developments in the markets and is then ready for a meeting with research staff, advising them on the implications of economic news. The rest of his day is filled with 'phone calls from clients and further meetings. And he really thrives on the stress. But he does also confess that you have to be fit to stay on top of a job like that.

> I haven't time for going to a gym or taking saunas, but I get a good sweat on walking briskly back homewards at night. I ring up and tell Chad, my neighbour, just where to pick me up. Some nights I walk further than others. It gives me

a breathing space for ideas to come and go. And by the time I've had a shower at home I'm ready for anything. I can't understand why more people don't walk more than they do.

Perhaps they do. There are more fleet of foot fortune-makers about than he thinks. And it is not only athletic young men and women in their mid-thirties, who are walking their way to success.

Walking to Success

In Britain there is a good example of one who is walking to success, in 59-year-old Sir Peter Thompson, a man with a string of 'Businessman of the Year' awards. He too is a great urban walker. It is his way of keeping physically and mental-ly fit for the 16-hour stint ahead of him each day. For the last 8 years he has been conceiving, orchestrating and bringing to a massively profitable fulfilment, one of the most remarkable projects of his time.

Exactly eight years ago, Peter Thompson was a manager in one of Britain's least glamorous, problem-plagued, state industries — the National Freight Corporation which embra-ced the Pickfords and British Rail parcel delivery services. It had such a dismal, loss-making record that it was right on the top of the Government's list for privatisation; a business they were prepared to get rid of at any price, it seemed.

Peter Thompson moved quickly, fleet of foot you might say, and together with the 11 other managers worked out a plan to buy the whole outfit, and let the 29,000 workforce participate by offering them shares.

Together, managers and workers took the plunge and financed the launch of their own freight firm with their own money. Now it is one of the most successful employee-controlled firms in the country. And talking of his workers today, Sir Peter says 'They act as if they owned the business — because they do. And how lucratively too!'

The shares they bought in 1982 for one pound each are now worth 56 pounds! Some former tanker-drivers have already retired to comfortable tax-haven homes in the Isle of Man sitting on a fortune of over £200,000.

As Chief Executive of this fast-growing business, Peter Thompson knows he has got to keep in top gear physically and mentally. Being in the driving seat of big business is no place for anyone who lacks the drive and vitality that goes with good health.

Like Irwin Kemp, Sir Peter has his own way of keeping fit. His chauffeur is instructed to drop him five miles from the office each morning so he can walk himself into the mood for the double day's work ahead.

He has walked his way not only to fitness, but also to bringing about one of the most remarkable industrial transformations of recent years.

Solving Problems and Making Decisions

So many people today are finding that walking is the most natural way to exercise for a healthy body and a lively mind. They are following the examples of the ancient Greek Philosophers, Aristotle and Plato, both dedicated walkers, who frequently spoke about the way that walking improved the mind's ability to think clearly and make decisions.

Businessmen today find that walking helps them to get problems in perspective. A senior executive of BP who walks part of his way to work each morning said: 'That early morning walk sets me up for the day. Somehow priorities fall into place. It's not that I'm deliberately thinking about work as I walk but somehow ideas just fall into an order of importance — those I can leave for a moment and those that I must deal with right away.'

A college vice-principal parks his car outside the city centre and walks to his office whether it is wet or fine. 'I would not miss that walk for anything. It gives me an uplifting injection. Like a stimulating drug, that sets me up for the day. By the time I am sitting at my desk I can make decisions more easily. My mind is clear, my lungs are free and aerated. I feel ready to consider memoranda and make decisions.'

Such personal experiences are supported by scientific research. A study carried out at Purdue University looked at 40 men and women aged between 27 and 66 years who recently took part in a fitness walking programme. The researchers found that those who exercised regularly improved their decision-making performance by 60 per cent over those who took no exercise.

Creativity

The great thinkers and writers throughout recorded history have enthused about walking, spoken of its magic and how it can transform both body and mind. Poets and novelists such as Emerson, Thoreau, Hazlitt, Goethe, Stevenson, Dickens, Jefferies, Burroughs, Ruskin and Coleridge were all great walkers. They too spoke of exercise being like a drug.

Stevenson declared: 'To all who feel overwhelmed and work weary, the exhilarating exercise of walking offers both a stimulus and a sedative'. And De Quincy told of how walking was responsible for much of Wordsworth's fine work. 'I calculate, upon good data, that Wordsworth's spindly legs must have traversed a distance of 175,000 miles, a mode of exertion which stood in the stead of alcohol and all other stimulants and we are indebted to this for much of what is excellent in his writings.'

Walking gives writers, artists, statesmen and -women time for creative thought.

A walk mid-morning or at midday can be most refreshing and productive. Leo Kessler, a prolific writer of fiction whose books have sold over 3,000,000 copies, is a dedicated urban walker, and is a man who could not manage without his breaks for walking. He lives in York, one of Europe's most beautiful cities, and never misses a day without walking its streets. He has this to say about his walks.

'I'm sure walking refreshes your mind as well as your body. After a long spell at the typewriter I set off round the city at a moderate pace — just enough to make me suck in air more deeply — and whilst one part of my brain is wondering how, in chapter nine, I can get the celebrated SS Colonel von Dodenburg of the Assault Regiment Wotan out of a tight corner in the desolate snow-bound High Vosges, another part of my mind is concerned with the architectural variations in the city's fine buildings. I'm a great believer in looking at things above eye-level. There you can find features most people miss. By the time I've done a tour of the city's alleys and passages I've probably also worked out how to get the Colonel into the exotic boudoir of the pistol-packing blonde Gräfin von Falken-stein in Chapter 10.'

There are numerous examples of writers who dash out for a quick walk when they reach a block in their narrative. Dean Swift, anticipating the modern faith in urban walking, used to put down his pen every two hours and walk the half mile up the hill near Temples and back again. At weekends he thought nothing of walking the 38 miles from Farnham to London.

For people like writers, artists and an ever-increasing number of computer operators working at home, going out into the city streets is something which can require a daily decision unless the walk is fixed for a regular time each day, so that habit can take over. The day's programme can then revolve around this fixed point. City commuters on the other hand have no such decisions to make, they will be on the streets at the same time every weekday morning and evening. And this is where the urban walker scores heavily over those who take other forms of exercise. It is the one fact that makes walking one of the best of all exercises for men, women, girls and boys; you can do it easily every day, week in, week out.

We know that for exercise to be beneficial it must be done regularly. Sessions of aerobic exercise often leave you with inactive intervals in between, and sometimes these intervals become longer than you intend because of bad planning or pressing commitments from elsewhere. Regular urban walking brings its own rewards year after year; of some of these you are not aware until you compare yourself with others of a similar age, and find you look younger and act in a sprightlier manner.

Busy people often advise others to try walking more. Member of Parliament, Sir James Spicer, who is also head of a big business group, says:

> As far as London is concerned, I am absolutely convinced that far too many people travel on public transport relatively short distances. It is faster on foot because of the traffic jams and they would gain tremendously from taking the additional exercise.
>
> Equally, in a large number of cases the two or three mile journey from home to work could be done just as quickly on foot as by public transport, particularly in the rush hour. I feel quite strongly about this.

In the forefront of American politicians who found walking in the city stimulating, were Presidents Jefferson, Lincoln and Truman. The latter was well-known for taking his brisk early morning walks in the neighbourhood of the White House with a pack of press-corps reporters and cameramen scurrying behind him.

There must be something in the practice of urban walking for so many successful people to recommend it, people who do not have time to spare and need to make the most of every minute. Try it for yourself. You will be surprised how you are able to get many more things done. It's almost like having a car engine tuned up; it works more efficiently. You will also find, strangely enough, that the time you spend walking is not at the expense of time for your family and friends, your hobbies or recreations. You will end each day feeling better about what you have been able to accomplish, and look forward to the next day's work without concern.

A Tip from Germany

'It's all very well talking about people who regularly have to travel to some fixed place of work, but what about all those who just have to be behind the wheel of a car, driving great distances, covering whole areas where they are agents and field representatives? What about us?' said a friend who is responsible for an area half the size of England in which he sells fertiliser and seeds to farmers.

Well, there is a method already provided as an example in Germany where walking is given tremendous publicity. The hard-working reps who think nothing of making calls 300 or 400 kilometres apart can pull off the autobahn into special exercise areas with signs leading to walks through the countryside. The signs are clearly set out and read *Trim dich Pfad* (roughly 'keep trim').

As they take a break from driving, men and women can walk along these pathways and, if they feel energetic enough, can swing from beams, chin themselves, let their vertebrae stretch and then walk on.

Kurt Heller, a 52-year-old representative from the great printing and publishing firm of Bertelsmann, is so keen on walking that he always carries a change of footwear with him in the car so that when he arrives for his business meetings he does not have to clean the mud from his shoes.

That change of scene, the exercise that pushes new blood through the whole of the body makes me arrive feeling livelier than if I had been slumped behind the steering wheel for four hours. And furthermore, I'm sure it is safer to make such a break, to relieve tensions and frustrations. People change once they have been behind the steering wheel for any length of time and I know that I am in a much better state of mind to do business when I get to my destination than if I had not taken a walk. I think a lot of my success is due to this habit of regularly taking walking breaks during the day.

It is not only the high flying executives and super sales people who are using walking to help them succeed. John Peacock is a fireman, an ambitious man too, who gave up teaching in order to earn more money. He gets annoyed when he hears people say that firemen sit around all day playing cards waiting for a call-out.

His divisional fire station in the Midlands has over 2,000 calls to respond to every year. And when he is not out fighting fires he is inspecting hydrants and doing any number of other essential jobs.

And, of course, firemen have to keep fit.

We have an hour's physical training every day in the new multi-gym and we used to go out running. I liked that. A fire tender followed to pick up the slow ones and to bring us all back quickly in case we got an alarm. But even then we sometimes got 'caught out' and so we had to stop the running. It was then that I hit upon this great idea.

I was at the time studying for promotion and yet wanted to get outdoors on my off-duty days. So I combined both these aims. In the evenings I made notes from my study books, read them onto a cassette and then when I went out walking I listened to them on my portable cassette player. I learnt, I kept fit, and kept alert all at the same time. It paid off, as you can see, I got my promotion.

Some people who take no physical exercise at all, come home in the evenings tired and never seem to get anything done.

'I once felt like that every night,' said Joan Davies, a civil servant working for the Ministry of Defence in Whitehall.

One day I realised that most of the men in the section did not go back up to the office after eating their midday meal, but donned their bowler hats and went out into St. James' Park. There you could see them striding out in their dark suits chatting happily away to one another.

I decided to go out too. At first I just went for the fresh air. I watched a 90-year-old man who came every day into the park carrying a bag full of old bread. The sparrows would sit on his head, shoulders, knees and arms, gobbling up the crumbs as he talked to them. Eventually I got tired of just sitting and took to walking. Before very long I was walking with my Head of Department. We didn't always talk shop and there was nothing more to our walking than just a friendly chat between like-minded souls. However, whether it was this friendship or just the walking that made me more efficient I don't know. But I got moved up a grade.

Obviously, at the end of the day, success is usually earned. It goes to those who are dedicated, often single-minded and have the mental and physical stamina to keep going and get things done. They are not tired before the end of the day. Things are not too much of a hassle for them, because they are firing on all six cylinders. Such people don't have to say, 'I haven't time', they can always make time.

Spinoza pointed the way. 'So long as man imagines that he cannot do this or that, so long he is determined not to do it; and consequently, so long it is impossible to him that he should do it.'

Finding the Time

Let me give you one more example of how successful men and women find time to walk because it benefits both their health and their career.

At the age of 35, Jack Hastings was a moderately successful salesman, but seemed to have reached a plateau in his career, until one day, shortly after he had pulled off a big sale and his confidence was at a high point, he decided that even though it was getting late in the day he would make a final call on a tough and difficult prospect.

To his surprise he made another big deal.

Now what has this to do with walking? Let Jack Hastings explain.

> What I remember most was that I was feeling good, confident and lively. My enthusiasm was great. I was thinking of my success earlier in the day and I identified the conditions which led to that success so that I could capitalise on them in the future. It was in that buoyant state of mind that I met my hitherto half-feared prospect. I was in command more than ever before. I convinced him to buy.
>
> Profiting from that experience I began to walk more often, rehearsing in my mind success stories as I walked, bolstering my confidence and enthusiasm. You can't do that driving a car. Your mind is on other things. Cluttered. And you've got to be physically active to 'hype' yourself up to a 'high'! And I find with walking, as the runners find with running, that the physical exertion actually gives you this high feeling. The adrenalin starts coursing through your blood, your heart is thumping and you believe in yourself and others believe in you.
>
> But there is another aspect to all this. When you come away from a job having pulled off a good deal you're feeling chuffed with yourself, the adrenalin is still running and you need time to unwind, to calm down before you get into your car and stuck in a snarl of traffic. It's a pity to waste that feeling of exhilaration in a car; I'm sure it's a feeling that's good for you because you feel so good, and you can benefit from it more if you walk back to your office or the place you've parked your car far enough away from the place where you've been doing business.

We can all profit from the experience of Jack Hastings. We can all take time to remind ourselves as we walk, of everything we are capable of doing, and have done successfully. Nothing succeeds like success, and we must make time to relish it. What better way than walking?

Then we too could find favour with Fortune perhaps.

8

The Urban Family Walk

'To Hell with it, I'm going for a walk. But if I'd done it halfway through writing this I would probably have got it done in half the time.'

Katharine Whitehorn, 'The Observer'

How many families are there these days which match the traditional, story-book or television advertisement family of one father working, one mother at home all day baking cakes and preparing meals and two well-groomed children racing eagerly home to a sit-down meal round a neatly laid table in a sparklingly polished home?

The question was put to executives of national companies at a meeting to discuss targeting the market. Some of these keen marketing men guessed that 75 per cent of families conform to this model; some cautiously guessed that there are about 25 per cent. The answer, in Britain, is actually 5 per cent.

Families are not what they used to be. Family life is far from what the glossy magazines would have us believe. For one thing, families seem to be spending less and less time together. The situation is the same in America as it is in Western Europe. Myra Hickman of Wisconsin is not unique in saying: 'The only time our family sits down together for a meal is at Thanksgiving and Christmas.' Timothy and Barry Lane of Birmingham said: 'We couldn't sit down together if we wanted to — unless we sat in a line on stools at the kitchen breakfast bar. We have our meals on trays that fit on the arms of our chairs so that we can watch television whilst we are eating.' No doubt there are many families like that too.

But if they do not meet together for a meal, when do they have time to be together and talk? Some families have found the ideal answer. They walk together. Mike Johnson, father of a boy aged ten and a girl of eight, says: 'Walk together and you stick together.' At least he also knows that the children are getting some useful exercise and developing an interest in a leisure pursuit which will last them a lifetime. And they will all, as a family be able to do well at walking. There are no winners and no losers.

Action Needed

There was a time when we could say that children always got enough exercise; they played boisterous games in the street, on the recreation ground and even round the lamp post on dark evenings. There were trees to be climbed, ropes to be skipped, dens to be built and wars to be fought. At school there were matches mid-week and on Saturday mornings; soccer, rugby and hockey in winter; cricket, swimming, netball and tennis in the summer.

But now schools have difficulty raising senior teams for a Saturday match. Older pupils have weekend jobs, stacking shelves in supermarkets, helping in garden centres or sitting behind the check-out tills in shops. Few are engaged in healthy strenuous physical activity. 'We've got to work to earn our pocket money,' said one skinny, brown-coated lad collecting trolleys in a Sainsbury supermarket car park.

And what of all that running about youngsters used to do in the evenings after tea? Few now go outdoors at all. Indeed, how safe is it for them to go out when newspaper delivery boys and girls carry alarm gadgets in case they are molested or attacked? Consequently, all too many youngsters spend most of their evenings sitting watching television or doing their homework. Clearly, children today do not get as much exercise as they used to have. They do not even have to walk to school any more; they travel in buses or their parents' cars. So this little bit of exercise has also been taken away from them.

This lack of physical activity among children has led to grave concern by health authorities, and current research reveals alarming evidence that precursors of coronary heart disease are already being found in young boys and girls.

In a project backed by Exeter University, Neil Armstrong and Jo Williams are studying the life-styles of 600 boys and girls aged between 11 and 16 years attending Queen Elizabeth Community College, Devon. They are finding their fears justified. 'It has been known for some time that these precursors of coronary heart disease had been found in young children,' said Jo. 'We are now gathering material which might reveal the causes, for example of the abnormally high levels of cholesterol recorded.' (This cholesterol was of the HDL variety and therefore not such a cause for anxiety, but still a condition which needed investigation.)

Part of this research involves attaching sensitive radio receivers to a belt worn by the children as they go about their work and play over a period of 12 hours. These receivers pick up the heart rate and transmit it to a watch worn round the pupil's wrist. For every 12-hour period the intensity of physical activity is measured. Bouts of extended muscular exertion are shown in terms of its duration in minutes and the increase in heart rate is recorded. The data are already providing some surprises.

'It has always been assumed that children are physically active, but what the data so far reveal is that these children of a small Devon market town are living comparatively sedentary lives,' said researcher Jo Williams. 'Hardly any of these children ever spend periods of more than five minutes a day when the heart rate is elevated to a level high enough to provide purposeful training and healthy physical development.'

One might wonder where all this inactivity is leading young people today. They seem to be heading for a condition that would make them suitable candidates for taking over from their parents in what has now been called the 'heart attack capital of the Western World' — Britain.

It is indicative of the state of unfitness of 18-year-olds today that the British Army has to reject four out of every ten of those who volunteer for service. 'They are so unfit they would never respond to the training and therefore would never reach the standard of military fitness which we require,' said a head-shaking Army recruiting major.

A British Army physical training specialist said that the situation was particularly bad in young men coming from State comprehensive schools where little importance is placed upon games and fitness training. Cadets selected for training at Sandhurst were of a high standard; they were young men drawn mainly from Public Schools where traditional games and sports were time tabled for Wednesday and

Saturday afternoons, and were well prepared physically for what they knew would be a tough course.

Here then is a problem for parents to face. And solve.

Worried Parents Find the Answer

Many parents are now giving serious thought to the problem. They see their children being brought up to lead sedentary lives and know that they may have to pay the price for this inactivity later in life in the form of degenerative diseases. Consequently they are taking action to inculcate habits of exercise in children at an early age, a time when children should be vigorously active. These far-sighted parents see one sure way of solving the problem of lack of physical activity. They are going out together, walking.

Parents too have suffered from inactivity in the past. And it is not always their fault. When today's parents went to school, much emphasis was placed on team games on the grounds that they were an effective way of developing attitudes of sportsmanship and fair play as well as giving large numbers of children exercise at the same time. But what happened when these youngsters left school was that very few bothered to join sports clubs so that they could continue playing the team games they had learnt. Seldom had these people been taught individual games like squash, badminton, or even tennis.

Consequently these people, the parents of today's children, lost the habit of taking exercise and became armchair sportsmen and women. The old adage of 'like Father, like son' then operated. Just as children of parents who smoke often follow their example, so the children of inactive parents may likewise grow up inactive. Now the adage is being put to positive use. Parents are taking exercise in the form of walking and their children are going with them.

An Activity for Everyone

Of all the possible sports activities not one of them can measure up to walking as an activity which can be shared so enjoyably and equally by a family together. The level of intensity is such that it can suit all ages with little modification.

Walking is something everyone can do well. You cannot

say this about any other sport. We know from experience that just as there is no such thing as the average man or woman that there are sports that suit some body-types more than others. For example, the tall, angular athlete with only a sparse covering of flesh on the bones is likely to do well in middle and long-distance running events and in non-body-contact sports. Whilst at the other end of the body-type spectrum we have the broad-framed individual well-covered with flesh and muscle who can outstrip all opposition in sports such as swimming and water-polo and yet finish last in a cross-country race.

However, when it comes to the activity of walking, no distinction can be made between body-types. It is an ideal sport for anyone at any age and is therefore particularly suitable as a family activity. Children, teenagers, or older members of the family need never feel frustrated because they are not making progress. The pace can be adjusted so that they can keep up with their friends and the rest of the family.

The Choice is Yours

Mark Hapgood should have been a doctor and by now be living in a comfortable executive-style house with one of those prestigious, highly priced cars we see advertised in the glossy magazines. At school he was what the teachers called a 'high-flyer' and what his friends called a 'lucky so-and-so' who could pass exams with only a bit of quick revision the night before. No one ever called him a book-worm or a swot possibly because he was always out at night and at weekends. In winter he was playing rugby or training for it and in the summer it was cricket.

Unfortunately for Mark Hapgood, one year in the last match of the rugby season, he became one of the statistics about which a Consultant Orthopaedic Surgeon wrote in a letter to *The Times* of 9th March 1988. Mark broke his leg: a bad fracture of the upper thigh which had to be pinned and plated. During those last few vital weeks leading up to his Advanced Level examinations which he would have to pass with high grades to achieve his place at Medical School, Mark Hapgood was in no fit state to study. He failed badly.

Now he is a hard-working, personable young man who can be seen limping up to people's houses in the evenings, a 'financial consultant' selling insurance.

It is true that there are some risks which do have to be taken in life, and there is perhaps a time and a place for them. But when choice has to be made it should be made in full knowledge of the facts.

Consultant Orthopaedic Surgeon, Mr Pringle, gave some idea of what such facts might amount to in his letter about about a quiet weekend in February when his 'clinic produced its usual quota of pain, economic hardship, and permanent disability'.

He wrote that, 'Of the 31 new patients, 14 of them had sustained sports injuries and there were in addition three emergency admissions from the playing fields which made a total of 17 injured sports persons in all. Of those, three required urgent surgery and others will come to surgery in due course.'

Such is the size of the sports injuries problem that Mr Pringle suggested that all sports players should be insured against these 'self-inflicted' injuries.

'The introduction of compulsory sports medical insurance with a no-claim bonus would encourage people to take better care of their bodies,' he wrote.

Mark Hapgood and many like him would probably be happier today if they had chosen a safer way to keep fit and healthy. Walking has much to offer, be it in the country or in an urban situation.

Pulling Together

Walking can pull families together as they learn to enjoy the discovery of so many delights as one unit; take Frank and Jennifer Dee for example. They bought a cottage in Cumbria when their three children were toddlers. Both Frank and Jennifer worked in the city of Manchester and were keen urban walkers. Jennifer always walked her children to school, rarely using the car, even in bad winter weather. At weekends they all looked forward to walking in the hills around their country cottage. As the children grew, so the distances they walked increased, though even at only five years old those children were walking much further than many adults could walk today.

Now Frank is 73 years old and Jennifer is still '39' or thereabouts, and they continue to walk together as a family. A happy and healthy family.

Walking and Talking

Naturally, when you are walking with your family or friends there is an opportunity for talking too, and so the activity becomes not only a beneficial form of exercise, but a social occasion also. Frank is sure about the importance of this:

> You get to know each other more, you make jokes, you make mistakes, you get lost and admit you're a fool, you break down barriers and learn how to confide in one another, you reminisce. We never had any of this nonsense of the generation gap that crept into the vocabulary of the sixties.
>
> And when I talk of confiding I don't just mean that my children confided in me. Often I was confiding in them. I told them of fears I had now and fears I had as a boy. So did Jennifer. You've got to give before you can take. When you're walking with half your mind on the things you are passing — buildings or mountains — you can talk with the other half of your mind. At times we unburdened ourselves without any feelings of embarrassment. Walk together often enough and inhibitions disappear.

Touching and Stroking

Psychologists frequently remind us that touching, cuddling and stroking are of the utmost importance to physical and mental well-being. They use this knowledge when treating patients in therapy sessions and recommend that families walking together make use of opportunities for such external signs of their affection for each other as touching, holding arms and hands and of putting an arm protectively round someone at times.

Dr Bertram Forer, in the journal, 'Psychotherapy' once wrote: 'The primitive reaction to being touched gently at critical periods is a feeling of body relaxation and assurance that one is not alone, that feelings of unworthiness are not justified.'

The innate need for stroking — both physical and verbal — which is innate in everyone from birth, is also stressed in Eric Berne's books *Games People Play* — the psychology of human relationships, and if ever there was a need for improving human relationships within the family and beyond it is now.

Children, particularly teenagers, often bottle up their feelings and back away from contact with parents and even friends, reluctant to say what is irritating them. Dr John Bonn, consultant psychiatrist at St Bartholomew's Hospital, is convinced that people of all ages should lighten their problems by talking them through. He believes we should use physical contact and relearn how to touch without embarrassment.

The urban family can profit much from opportunities for touching. If they stop occasionally there is a chance for touching and pointing upward to some feature of interest, stooping lower to put the face close to a child's to show pleasure and excitement in discovering and watching something together. Such physical contact is natural, healthy, and beneficial to both parent and child.

Walking and Learning

As you walk together in an urban environment you learn together. And one thing that an urban walking family will learn is independence and self reliance. Children need not grow up believing that a car is essential. You can encourage and teach young people to think for themselves and work out alternatives to the car as a means of travel by having a day set aside when the car is off the road except for emergencies. Children can then grow up with a far better knowledge of how to get about their own locality and even further afield. They could easily derive more excitement from this than from being passively driven everywhere. But it is important that hazards are explained and safety precautions stressed. We live in dangerous times and we must learn how to survive.

Parents can play an important part in this learning process through active discovery. Some parents walk with their baby in a sling and toddlers taken by the hand, continuing like this until the child is tired. He is then carried for a while before walking a little further. Health and happiness start with the family, and parents can at this early age lay down the foundations for healthy habits which will pay dividends in later life. In walking together you can learn not only the advantages of taking regular exercise, but also how to adjust to a group and keep talking as you walk.

Family walks, though, have to be fun. It is no use badgering children to go for a walk, they have to be led. Vary the route, heighten their awareness of their surroundings, let them see and wonder at all the curious things made by men and women over vast stretches of time.

Listen to the suggestions made by your children, support their ideas, let them learn from experience.

Safe Walking

When a family with young children starts walking together you have an ideal opportunity for teaching road safety and reinforcing those safety codes promoted by education authorities and the media.

In addition to all the advice available you can stress to young children the need to do the following:

- Walk on the opposite side of the road to the traffic, facing the oncoming traffic, so they can see you and you can see them.
- Wear brightly coloured clothing or luminous safety belts and bands when walking at night or in conditions of poor visibility.
- Keep well away from the road and clear of the kerb. Trucks in heavy traffic can drive perilously close to pedestrians.
- Cross the road at traffic lights or at recognised crossing points whenever possible.
- Look both ways twice before stepping out into the road and make sure there is time to cross at walking pace; do not run.
- Watch out for irresponsible oncoming pedestrians who might force you to step off the pavement onto the road.

All things considered, you must agree that there is much to be gained from urban walking as a family. You will be laying the foundation for the good health and happiness of your own family and for their children as well.

9

The Urban Walker's Exercise Supplement

'And perhaps the reward for the spirit who tries
Is not the goal but the exercise'

Edmund Vance Cooke in the prayer, 'The Uncommon
Commoner'

There has never been a time in the history of the world when
men and women have been more informed about their own
health and the potential hazards they face, than they are
today. Scarcely a week goes by without some newspaper
carrying a report on a new discovery for the treatment of
some illness, or of a new risk we are running. We are
bombarded with advice and with a wide variety of exercise
schedules each promising to safeguard our most priceless
possession — our good health.

Do walkers need to bother with such routines?

The simple answer is 'No'. Walkers can get by, be perfectly
healthy, and live to a great age without ever doing a press-up
or trunk curl. The exercise from walking will develop all the
cardio-vascular and respiratory efficiency you need for good
health. But does that mean you will be fit?

Before we can answer that question we must be clear in our
minds about the nature of fitness and how it is relative to the
task to be tackled. It is easy to see, for example, that the
heavy-weight boxer needs a different kind of fitness from the
squash player or sprinter. Each may be physically fit in his
own way, but each is in a different physical condition. We are
not concerned here with fitness for Olympic athletes or
international sportsmen and women, but for life in general.
But varying degrees of fitness may be required and no two
individuals are alike in their needs for physical development

or rehabilitation after a long period of inactivity or sickness. And in recognising these different needs we can adapt conditioning programmes to provide us with our own individual training programme.

Whilst walking provides excellent exercise for two thirds of the muscle mass of the body (which is in the legs) and makes adequate demands upon the heart and lungs for their development, it cannot give all the exercise needed for total body fitness. To achieve this we need to exercise all the major muscle groups of the body. This does not mean to say that we should be working towards bulging biceps, massive pectorals and rope-like striations of the abdominals, but should do just enough exercise to keep them in trim. Muscles are made to be used and if they are not, then they atrophy (they waste away). We have only to look at a leg that has been in plaster after a fracture and see how much thinner it is than its counterpart which has been able to use its muscles.

Another reason for a supplementary exercise programme for the urban walker is the mobility of joints. Did you ever bite your big toe as an infant? It's easy to do at that age. Can you do it now? It is hardly likely that you can, or that you would be any fitter even if you could, but we should aim for a reasonable degree of body flexibility.

The human body needs stretching exercises as well as strengthening ones; otherwise joints, muscles, tendons and ligaments lose their ability to function in their full range. You can see now why a few stretching and strengthening exercises can be of benefit even to fit walkers. But gently does it! Remember you are not aiming to become a contortionist, ballet dancer or top-class gymnast, and if you have been leading a fairly sedentary life then you should not suddenly start doing those rhythmic mobilising, Scandinavian-type exercises that your gym teacher at school might have put you through some years ago.

The natural, safe way to become fit for most of the physical demands of life is to progress gradually – you will have noticed by now how often this phrase, 'progress gradually' has been used. If you overdo the exercises you might not feel like walking afterwards.

Warm up for the exercises for a few minutes and you will derive more benefit from them. These exercises should stretch the major muscle groups and work all joints through their full range of movement. Select a few of the exercises listed below and do them until they promote a feeling of general warmth and a little perspiration, accompanied by an increase in the rate and depth of respiration.

Suggested Programme of Exercises for Maintaining Joint Mobility

Double arm circling: stand with your feet apart and swing your arms loosely overhead passing close to your ears, behind the line of your shoulders and forward again. Keep your wrists, elbows and shoulders relaxed the whole time.

Ski swings: with your feet about six inches apart, swing your arms loosely and rhythmically backwards and forwards and upwards, at the same time bending and stretching your knees as you might in skiing movements.

Kneeling press-ups: kneel on the floor with your head as close to your knees as you can and your bottom on your heels. Stretch your arms out forwards on the floor in front of your head. Raise your body now so that your shoulders are above your hands and your thighs vertical so that your hips are directly above the knees. Bend your arms so that your chin touches the floor. Straighten your arms and return to the starting position.

Trunk twisting: stand with your feet apart and your arms forward with fingers lightly clenched, at shoulder height. Keeping the body upright, twist round to the left and then to the right. Allow your arms to swing loosely round with your body and turn the head to look as far round as you can. (This is a good exercise for those who have difficulty looking round when reversing a car!)

Straight leg swinging: stand with one leg close to a wall and the outside leg raised off the ground so that it can be swung easily forwards and backwards. Maintain your balance by resting one hand against the wall. You could do this exercise resting one hand upon a chair back instead of a wall. Keeping the leg as straight as possible try 10 swings with the left and then 10 with the right. You will feel the hamstrings being stretched. Be careful not to do this exercise too violently.

Knee hugging: stand on one leg. Raise the other, pulling the knee close to the chest. Hugging first the left leg and then the right, do as many as you feel necessary.

Arm and trunk circling: stand with your feet apart and with your arms straight and clasped loosely overhead. Using the hips as a pivot, sweep your whole body with arms extended in a wide circle, sideways, upwards and backwards, sideways and down across the feet. Feel the pull at the hips all the way round. Continue circling in a smooth rhythm.

Neck rotation: drop your head onto your chest, circle over the left shoulder, backwards and down over your right shoulder.

A Word of Warning about Mobilising Exercises

Do not be over-enthusiastic about mobilising joints and muscles. Pick the exercises that give you pleasure and then you are more likely to do them more often. Follow the guidelines set out below:

- Do not force any joints or muscles beyond a comfortable range of movement.
- Move slowly and deliberately.
- Never bounce or use excessively rhythmic movements of the body to extend the range of movement.
- Do the exercises in any order you like.
- Continue each movement until you see a slight discomfort in the part of the body being stretched.

Stretching

'Walking is my hobby, exercise, medicine and profession. It is my life.' These are the opening words in the book written by a man who has toured all the American states preaching the gospel of walking, Robert Sweetgall. In addition to all the other advice he gives to those who are about to start walking for their health, he says that 'Stretching is an important part of a walking programme. Many other sportsmen and women believe in stretching before strengthening. Weight trainers in particular believe that time spent stretching is never time wasted. Try some of the exercises they recommend.'

Stretching Exercises

Shoulder girdle stretch: raise your right arm and reach behind your neck to touch the back of the left shoulder. Lift your left arm and apply a gentle pressure on to the top of the right elbow, pressing it a little further down.

Hurdle stretch: sit down on the floor, with your right leg stretched forward and your left leg tucked as far back as you can, let your body lie slightly backwards supported by your arms. Feel the muscles stretching as you move your body.

Quadriceps stretch: lie on your right side with your right arm extended along the floor beyond the head and your right leg straight. Reach down with your left hand and gently pull your left leg backwards, bending at the knee, drawing your heel towards the buttock. Hold the leg in this position for a few seconds until you feel the quadriceps muscles along the front of the thigh being stretched. Let the leg return to the starting position and then repeat the exercise. Change sides and legs. There are variations of this exercise. It can be done from a standing position with your body leaning forward and one hand resting on the wall for support while the free hand is used to pull one leg backwards.

Back arching: support your body, cat-like on all fours with your legs straight. Walk your feet forwards as far as you can, arching your back high. Now walk forwards with your hands, and then lower your hips to the floor, letting your feet slide back so that your back and neck form a concave arch.

Remember when you are doing mobilising and stretching exercises to listen to what your body is telling you. If you have an ache or pain or don't feel up to a session of exercise, especially if you are elderly, then settle for a shorter session. Exercising should be fun, not an ordeal: gently does it!

Strengthening Exercises

Whilst one of the main aims of your urban walking programme must be to improve and maintain general cardio-vascular fitness, there is much to be gained from supplementing the walking exercise with special exercises designed to develop muscular strength in the upper body. Extra strength in the torso will contribute much to your enjoyment of urban walking.

It is true that the muscles of the shoulder girdle work hard in swinging the arms while you walk (and you could give them extra work by holding a small weight in each hand) and the muscles to the front and back of the body are constantly working to maintain your body in an upright position and in the posture required for good walking style, but the exercise involved tends to develop stamina rather than strength.

Consequently, to ensure harmonious development of the

whole body a few special strengthening exercises are desirable as a supplement to the whole programme.

It may be that the younger and fitter urban walker would like to take the supplementary strengthening routines in the form of weight training. But for most people there are exercises which achieve good results using the same principle of progressive resistance without having to go to a weight training gym. Adequate resistance is afforded through the use of gravity and body weight or with other items which are readily accessible, as will be seen from the list of exercises given below.

Once more, take care, let your build-up to greater demands on the muscular system be gradual, an undertaking of effort that is just that little bit more than you have been accustomed to and no more. Remember you are doing it for your own benefit, in your own time and at your own pace. You are not competing with anybody, not even yourself. If you feel any nausea, cramp or pain in the chest then stop right away and seek medical advice.

Suggested Exercises for Strengthening the Upper Torso

The sit-up with bent knee. Begin this exercise with your hands alongside the body as you lie on the floor with your knees together and bent, and your feet flat on the floor. Roll up to a sitting position. You can add to the severity of the exercise by holding your hands behind your head, and add more resistance still by holding a heavy book in your hands behind the neck. This is a very good abdominal exercise.

The high push-away. You can modify the starting position of this exercise to suit whichever degree of resistance you wish to apply to the muscles of the chest and extensors of the arm. Stand a little way from a solid table or desk, fall gently forwards to support your body weight on straight arms. Bend your arms until your chest or chin touches the desk then push away hard so that your arms are straight and your hands come right off the supporting table or desk.

Wall push-away. This is another exercise which enables you to develop muscle fibres by pitting your muscles against resistance, but in this case the effort needed is not as great as in the previous exercise because your body is in a more upright position and therefore your arms and chest muscles are not having to work against as much of the body's weight.

Stand about a yard away from a wall. Lean forwards and let your hands rest against the wall with the arms straight. Lower your body until your chest approaches the wall and then push away strongly to regain the starting position. Continue at this distance of an arm's length from the wall, and when you can complete 20 repetitions easily, then increase the resistance by moving your feet further back.

Press-ups, high and low. The usual press-up exercise is that done with the body supported by straight arms, hands shoulder width apart, body straight and supported also by the toes on the floor. The arms are bent and stretched in this position so that the nose touches the floor each time without the body bending or sagging at the hips.

Progression in this well-known exercise is achieved by raising the feet so that the toes rest on a chair and the body weight is supported by the hands on the floor. The arms are bent and stretched as in the usual exercise.

With the low press-up, the hands rest on a chair or box on each side of the body. Take your body-weight on your hands and toes keeping the whole body in a straight line with your legs; dip your chest through your arms and hands until your shoulders are level with your hands. Press up to regain the starting position. The high and low press-ups should be attempted only when adequate strength has been developed by the more conventional push-away and press-up exercises.

Special Exercises for the Back

Back pain can stop you walking. It's a pain that afflicts young and old alike and the symptoms associated with this pain account for more visits to the doctor than any other complaint.

Just as walking can help us to avoid heart disease, back exercises can help us to avoid incapacitating back pain.

You don't have to be a martyr to backache. Keep your back and abdominal muscles strong through regular, safe exercise and by taking precautions so that you do not over-stretch the small intervertebral muscles when you lift, carry and push.

Before you start these exercises remember that the short muscles and ligaments which retain the intervertebral discs in position are easily damaged by lifting heavy weights in a round-backed posture. The exercises below are those which work the dorsal muscles either at their normal length or from the normal length to a shortened one.

The back raise. Lie with your arms sideways, holding a light book in each hand. Raise the trunk and arms backwards at the same time. Brace your shoulder blades firmly together keeping your chin tucked in. You will find this exercise easier if you can anchor your feet beneath a heavy piece of furniture.

Variations of this exercise to bring greater resistance for the dorsal muscles, can be effected by holding a book behind your neck or at arm's length in front of the body.

The trunk curl. Lie on your back with your feet a little apart and your hands by your sides. Raise your head and shoulders until you can just see your ankles. This is the starting position. Now curl your body forwards and reach with your hands until you can just place your finger tips on the lower edge of the knee cap. *Do not sit right up.* Lower yourself down to the starting position, as above. Remember to keep your head and shoulders off the floor until all the repetitions have been completed.

Making Your own Programme

You can select one exercise for each part of the body and do each one as many times as you can until you notice signs of fatigue — or you can take one objective at a time. For example you could concentrate on strengthening your back muscles, then develop a trimmer waist line and firmer abdominals. Step by step you can improve all the parts of your body without feeling that you are undertaking a chore. In this way you can, in conjunction with your urban walking programme, improve your heart and lungs and reshape your body, making it leaner, fitter and healthier. Diet and walking will remove excess pounds and exercises will remove the inches by making your muscles firmer. The key to success with walking and with the supplementary exercise programme is moderation. People who work themselves into a frenzy of enthusiasm at the start of a fitness campaign rarely carry it through, for no one can sustain such a pitch of dedication for a very long time. Settle for a steady though moderate rate of progress. Avoid the get fit quick fad routines that promise dramatic results, but often fail to deliver in the end.

Take it easily and steadily and you have it all.

Is it Worth the Effort?

The man or woman who exercises has, for centuries, been fair game for the supercilious scoff or snigger. There are quotations galore to ridicule the idea of taking exercise. The American writer, Mark Twain, is reported to have said that he took his exercise by following the funeral processions of those of his friends who exercised regularly. Playwright George Bernard Shaw had more than one dig at exercises too: 'Whenever I feel the need for taking exercise I go and lie down until the feeling passes off.'

Even now, when current medical research is constantly revealing more about the importance of exercise, there are still cynics who deride people who swipe a small white ball into the distant fairway and then trudge doggedly after it until they have sunk it down 18 small holes in the ground. And as for people who go to weight-training gyms, they are belittled by cynics quoting from Martial *Epigrams*, Book xiv:

Why do strong men fatigue themselves
With frivolous dumb-bells?
To dig a vineyard is worthier exercise for men.

But the scoffers cannot deny that in these days of automation, our daily tasks have become less physically arduous. Machines have been built to carry out the heavy work of most processes, but muscles were made to be used. Surely it is better to provide exercise for them than to let them disappear for lack of work?

But there is one argument in favour of exercise that needs no physiological training to appreciate and there is no contradiction possible. It is the glow of physical fitness that comes from peak condition and the satisfaction of the exercise itself. It is an old argument which was once described in verse by Edmund Vance Cooke in the prayer, 'The Uncommon Commoner':

'And perhaps the reward for the spirit who tries
Is not the goal but the exercise.'

10

The Delights of the City Walker

'A break in daily routine often can pep you up. Buy something new to wear, walk part of the way to work or find a new route. Since boredom breeds fatigue, discover new interests or activities. Enthusiasm for something new to be learnt or done builds up energy.'

Edward L Bortz MD

Not long ago, John Rogers had a problem. It led him to make a decision that he has not regretted.

'It was a complicated story involving divorce, terrifying bank statements, inserting my cash dispenser card with trepidation, expecting the machine to digest it. The culmination was bouncing standing orders for my life insurance linked to my mortgage!'

It took him a week to mull frantically over his chaotic finances. Suddenly, one day, with a flash of clear-sightedness — bolstered by idealism, concern for the environment and worry over pollution — he found the obvious solution. Sell the car. He took to his feet.

'And as for the rest of it,' said John, 'if you'll pardon the pun, I've taken it in my stride.' He mastered the arcane intricacies of the 1500 page British Rail timetable, learnt the differences between White-saver and Blue-saver days and let others drive him to work. He accustomed himself to budgeting time for walking, catching buses and even occasional taxis and now finds life full of delights.

'I can't help a smug smile when occasionally noticing the bus driver swearing under his breath at idiot car drivers cutting in front, suddenly pulling up, turning unexpectedly or parking in the bus lay-by.'

At the end of his working week he delights in the luxury of leaning back in his train seat, the *Daily Telegraph* crossword puzzle on the table in front of him and watching Britain whizz by at 80 mph. After drinks or snacks and occasional conversation, he arrives relaxed and ready for a pleasant weekend ahead.

It is comforting for him to feel a certain amount of self-righteousness in knowing that there is one person fewer hurtling a potentially lethal metal box along the motorway.

In terms of hard cash he estimates he is far better off financially than he would have thought possible. He spends about £1,000 on fares but has saved twice that on hire purchase payments, car running costs, insurance and so on. As he so convincingly said: 'Not to be sniffed at, is it?'

Looking and Finding

John Rogers is not alone. Hundreds and thousands of people like him, motivated by a variety of good reasons, are walking more and finding their lives enriched in more ways than one.

Janet Sinclair, a dynamic personal assistant to the chief executive of a prestigious Mayfair-based concern, talks enthusiastically of a wonderful new world of delight she has discovered. Every day she is finding marvels to wonder at in the city where she has worked now for 12 years.

> You never really know a place until you have walked about it. The view from the driving seat of a car or from the steamed-up windows of a London bus is nothing compared with all you can take in from the pavement. Since I started walking my life has been enriched in countless ways, and I don't mean just financially.

Give her half a chance and she will keep you enthralled for hours talking about her 'discoveries'. The story of the cock on the church will perhaps illustrate what I mean.

> I looked up at the church steeple I was passing one day and saw this rooster thing with a huge flared tail and I began to wonder how and why it got there. I'd seen weather-vanes on steeples — you know the sort of thing with an arrow and metal flag — but never a big gold cock. I wondered why they put a cock up there to show which way the wind

was blowing. It puzzled me all day and so on the way home that night I called in the church and found a curate to question. He was pleased to impart all his knowledge. He told me that the cock reminded the congregation and all who passed the church to be wakeful and watchful of all the sin about us. He then recalled that the cock had another significance. It was the crowing cock that had reminded St Peter of his denial of Christ.

Later that evening when Janet was sipping her hot coffee in front of the fire with her husband, a lecturer in English Literature at London University, she learnt something more about the weather-cocks on church steeples. In former times, her husband explained, the cock was thought to be a powerful bird which protected houses and shooed away evil spirits. He told her how in Shakespeare's play, *Hamlet*, the officer of the Danish Guard, Marcellus, reported that the ghost of Hamlet's murdered father faded on the crowing of the cock.

The next time Janet Sinclair passed that city church steeple she glanced upwards to see if the cock was still on duty protecting the parish.

The urban walker who looks perceptively about him cannot but wonder at the curious artifacts visible to the inquisitive eye in cities all the world over. This is surely not surprising when we read the latest statistics which show that 28 million tourists flock each year to Britain alone. Britain is now number five in the list of the world's most popular tourist attractions, drawing millions to rubber-neck as they walk through the streets ancient and modern.

For those who work and walk in the city every day, simple objects can stimulate the imagination and lead to all sorts of delights in the course of further investigation. This sort of enquiry can put you in touch with places, cultures, history, art and the wonders of the world. Urban walkers learn how to explore their surroundings in depth, using the five senses — stimulating their minds.

It can be like a new game of looking and finding, providing pleasure and delight at so little cost. It can lead you into local reference libraries, second-hand bookshops and museums. Further investigation might bring you into contact with local historical societies and their specialist contacts.

One keen 'looker' recalls being side-tracked once with a book which told of the delights of eating young pink moles dug up from the ground or very young pink rats pulled out of a stack of wheat (very doubtful delights). But then the book was written in the first world war when the writer thought that everyone was going to starve.

Tracking down Secrets

A little detective work in the public library can soon put you on the track of some of the mysteries of your own town or city. In the index of the county history you could find details of buildings, archaeology and local arts and crafts. The *Dictionary of National Biography* will tell you of any famous people who lived or worked in your area (saints, scientists, painters, explorers, inventors, novelists, soldiers, highwaymen, forgers or murderers). Many perhaps walked in the very area in which you walk.

Fortunately, many local authorities have adopted an excellent practice of putting plaques on buildings in which famous people lived or worked. In London, for example, the Council have placed chocolate coloured commemorative tablets on some houses and newer tablets are blue with white lettering. Constant research is ensuring that fresh tablets are affixed to newly discovered sites of interest. Here is another possible field for the urban walker to explore and become actively involved in: a source of satisfaction and delight.

When you are tracking down the secrets of the past, second-hand bookshops and reference libraries can play a useful part. In them you should be able to find large-scale maps — those with a scale of 2½ inches to the mile are ideal — which should show you more about your own locality than you ever imagined. If you can get hold of a map with a scale of 6 inches to the mile, that can be even better. Using a map like that you could start adding the details of your own discoveries. Make the map work for you: put your data on it boldly. Such maps are made to be used not kept as pictures.

Very soon the urban walker who is interested in his own environment can find a completely new interest in life and one that can make each day's walk a new journey of discovery.

The deeper you delve into the whys and wherefores of the urban scene the more interesting it all becomes. Your next step is to try and get hold of one of the very old Ordnance Survey maps, printed in about 1809 for the military. (The publishers, David and Charles of Newton Abbot, are now reprinting them.) Before long you could be walking the streets as they were before Wellington defeated Napoleon at Waterloo (the Belgian place and not the British Rail station). There is almost no end to such detective work. One clue leads to another and that to another.

You could, for example, ask the British Museum for a photocopy of the original surveyor's drawings from which the old maps were made. Armed with these sketches and maps you can walk through the city streets with an eye that is marvellously well-informed, searching for clues to the past.

How different such a morning's walk to work would be from the journeys of other city commuters hurrying through only the last few yards of their journey on foot. How much more healthy than a crowded and stuffy train or bus. How much more delightful!

Buildings are of tremendous interest to those who have taken time to know something about their architecture. But you don't need to be an expert to start enjoying looking and finding. The outward appearance of buildings can reveal much of the historical development of towns and cities. It is not always easy to give a precise date to them because many of the buildings are a mixture of styles with various features added to an existing older structure. But as you pass them on your walks, look more closely at them; note the grace and dignity of the big Georgian terraced houses which are so lacking in later Edwardian semis, learn how to recognise the pretentious Victorian mock-Gothic, look at the typical ribbon development of thirties-style small semis and the bigger bay-windowed ones of the well-to-do professional classes. See how in the process of change in towns, much of the past is preserved, but note also how, in many instances, little attention has been paid to the way that new buildings harmonise with the old. Consider how much evidence there really is for the frequent outbursts of HRH the Prince of Wales against the poor planning, poor conservation and poor workmanship within the inner cities.

These are *our* towns and cities. We are now a nation of town dwellers. The growth of the town population during the last 200 years means that over 80 per cent of the population lives in urban communities. It is up to us to look after them.

The American Institute of Architects advocates looking at

the architecture of all buildings — public, private and business — on foot, from a human perspective, as the best way to experience texture, scale, and distance. It is worthwhile to become more familiar with your own city, read about its history and architecture, then get outside and walk. You will then begin to enjoy your own environment more.

It is only right that everyone should be taking a greater interest in what the planners are doing. Neglect of this in the past has resulted in appalling decay; well-built houses have been allowed to fall into ugly disrepair.

Fortunately, as we explore the city on foot we can find delightful examples of whole areas which have been splendidly restored: in which people are now living and taking a pride in their environment. We always have to remember that towns are living things serving the needs of those of us who live and work in them; it is up to us to look hard at what is around us, to raise our voices against whatever is tasteless and dull, to appreciate and try to preserve the types of buildings that please the eye. There is obviously much in this field that could engage the active interest of the urban walker.

It is not, however, only the sights which can delight the city walker; the sounds and smells can stimulate the imagination too, for every city has its own peculiar blend. Consider how the character of a city can be conveyed by its aromas; the delicious smell of freshly roasted coffee and newly baked morning brioches wafting out of a Paris café, the roast pork on the spit, spiked with rosemary in midday Bologna, the spitting *Brathühnchen* and bursting *Bratwurst* on open stalls in Cologne and the sizzling *chuletas* in Marbella. How can you savour such flavours on a bus? The walker has all these riches and yet more.

There are the sounds of the city too; the calls of shopkeepers, the good-natured banter of the marketmen, the music of the buskers and the *mélange* of foreign languages, especially as you walk through the ethnic quarters of New York, Washington, London or Amsterdam. In diverse urban areas you can see such a mixture of dress and fashion that within a short space of time you have caught a glimpse of several different cultures.

There is no need to rely entirely on your own resources in exploring a city on foot. To supplement your usual route you could seek help to find alternative walks and interesting features of which you might never have heard.

Many cities have volunteer guides who, for no charge, will take you through the real, living history of the city streets and introduce you to new snickelways and alleys. In York, for example, these guides will take you through buildings planned and built by the Romans and Vikings, through the Middle Ages to the Georgians and Victorians. Within one square mile they will show you enough to excite the most hardened world-traveller.

In Zurich and Paris you can be led through the elegant shopping streets; in London guides will walk you along streets where Dickens strolled by the Inns of Court. In the USA you can follow the Freedom Train in Boston, or the historic Inner Harbour area of Baltimore; you can be guided through the crowded sidewalks of Vieux Carré in New Orleans and so on. St Louis has Sunday tours led by architects who point out the interesting features of buildings. These are but a few examples of what is available for you as you walk in the city.

Make full use of what is there for you to enjoy, the enchantment of looking into all the city has to offer, from its past history to its present developments.

Some cities offer self-guided tours which can be obtained from Information Centres. The New York City Museum provides lists of Sunday walking tours with various themes such as, 'Loft living and high art' or 'The world of Edith Wharton'. Or there are the cassette city tours. These taped tours allow you to walk at your own pace and for whatever distance you choose. You can stop whenever you feel like stopping, eat and drink whenever you wish to, and then carry on when you want to walk more. The earphones enable you to hear what the guide is saying without having to strain or push to the front to see what he is pointing out. More and more cities are preparing such tapes. They tell you historical anecdotes, give you the folk-lore and explain features of interest. They tell you which streets to walk along and when to turn off into another. As yet there is no central office in Britain from which you can obtain such tapes, but in America you can send for a free catalogue from: Travelcassettes, Box 8361, New Haven Ct.

You might think that you know your own city, but quite often those who live and work in a particular city say they never have time to visit all the places of interest. Why not start to find out more about your own town now by going to the nearest Information Centre and seeing what they have to offer in the way of maps and pamphlets? Decide to get to know your streets and buildings; plan your walking — and have fun.

11

The Way Back – Walking

In the hot summer of 1955, from Colorado, USA, came news that shocked the whole world. President Dwight D Eisenhower, champion of the free world and the West, had suffered a major heart attack. In March 1945 whilst he was at the height of his wartime power as Supreme Allied Commander in Western Europe mounting a major offensive against the Rhine, indications of his declining vigour were already evident. Although he was only 55 years old then, he could not walk upstairs to his headquarters at Rheims because of a bad knee and shortness of breath — (he smoked sixty Lucky Strikes a day) — and he was generally exhausted.

'Look at you,' said his Chief of Staff, 'You've got bags under your eyes. Your blood pressure is higher than it's ever been, and you can hardly walk across the room.'

He was secretly whisked away with his chauffeuse come mistress, Kay Summersby, to a very rich American's villa, 'Sous Le Vent' on the French Riviera near Cannes. There, for the first two days he did nothing but sleep, then he took short walks and within days he was back at his quarters. Revived. But for how long? Those who were close to him had grave doubts.

Eisenhower, though, was determined to become fit. He took more exercise. The war ended. He became Supreme Commander of North Atlantic Treaty Forces in Europe and in 1952 he was elected President of the USA. It was just before he was about to stand for a second term of office that he was struck down with a heart attack.

The American newspapers, with characteristic frankness, filled their columns with details of the President's convalescence while the public and the doctors debated whether he would be able to stand again. They had not reckoned with Ike's determination. He walked more, played golf, had a stomach operation and then, in the Spring of 1956, made his decision to run for President again. Despite his heart attack and the stomach operation he recovered his vigour, carried off a successful electioneering campaign and was returned to office with a majority of 10,000,000.

The point of this story is to illustrate the current attitude to heart attacks. At one time they spelt the end of the road for anyone carrying the responsibilities of high office. Eisenhower showed the way back to good health which is being followed more and more often. He walked back. Altogether he spent eight critical years in the White House during which he tried hard to convince the world, and particularly Mr Khrushchev, of the peaceful intentions of the USA. These were certainly not easy years. Finally he retired to his farm at Gettysburg, Pennsylvania and lived a healthy active life for many years before dying a few weeks short of his eightieth birthday. He had shown everyone the way back to active life after a heart attack — a walking way.

What is it Like to Have a Heart Attack?

A heart attack can be a very painful and frightening experience. It happened to a Manchester meat and food inspector I knew well. He had just retired, and a month or two later returned to the inspector's office at the City Abattoir to say hello to his old friends. Whilst he was standing talking to them he began to feel faint, slightly giddy and sick. Foolishly, because he did not want to be a nuisance, he bade goodbye to his friends and went out to the bus stop. There he leant against the wall, his face white, lips blue and almost collapsed when a sudden, crushing, vice-like pain gripped the centre of his chest. It spread alarmingly to his jaw, throat, arms and back. He never knew how he got home but somehow managed to arrive and then — another foolish mistake — crawled upstairs to bed. Fortunately the doctor came immediately and had him admitted to hospital.

There he rested and was reassured by the cardiac specialist and nurses of the coronary care unit, that most people could expect to return to living a fairly normal life within a few months — depending upon how severe the attack had been. He stayed in bed for a few days and was monitored by an electrocardiogram to show up any abnormalities in his heart beat. Then he was allowed to start moving again. He took his first short walk down the road. With a nurse beside him to give him confidence he began to walk a little further each day. Those walks were to get longer and longer as he made his way back to good health.

All that happened when he was sixty-two years old.

Before he left hospital the doctor gave him a carefully planned programme of activity designed to build up his strength gradually. At first he would take a gentle walk to the park where he would sit on a bench for a while, watching the bowls. As days and weeks went by he would try to walk further and further, enjoying the fresh air and also enjoying feeling more confident of his recovery.

No longer, though, did he eat the joints of beef that he had relished as a meat inspector, he ate more fresh green vegetables and fresh fruit and fish; he bought skimmed milk and cut out all sugar and fat. He also ate plenty of broad beans. He kept his weight down, did not smoke and was soon able to say: 'I feel fitter than I've done for years!'

His highly polished Ford Prefect stayed mainly in the garage; he walked to and from the shops and library almost every day, a good three miles, even when he was eighty.

He proved the point that you can walk to a happy and full life. I knew his routine well and know that he was not exaggerating when he said he felt fitter than he had felt for a long time as a result of his post-cardiac walking programme. I miss him now. He was my father.

Exercise after a Heart attack

It cannot be emphasised too much that those who have had a heart attack should take exercise only under the supervision of a cardiologist until given the go-ahead for a more ambitious programme. It is of critical importance not to start before the doctor has decided when you can exercise and how much you can do. Do not worry. He will be encouraging you to walk more and more as soon as he feels it is safe for you to do so.

There was a time when most heart specialists thought that cardiac patients should have as much bed rest as possible and even warned them about the risk involved in walking upstairs.

In the last 15 years medical thinking has changed a lot. Many doctors now advise their patients to begin walking a little at a time, as soon as they feel they have the strength to do so. Erika Sivarajan writing in the *New England Journal of Medicine* (13 August 1981) argued in this way: 'If one assumes that a sedentary life-style is a risk factor and that exercise is a desirable preventative measure, then starting an exercise programme during hospitalisation when patients are highly motivated may well help to establish a habit of exercise.'

Terence Kavanaugh MD of the Toronto Rehabilitation Centre has studied post-heart-attack patients being treated with exercise therapy and he believes that the best time to start such a programme would be after about 6 weeks. Most of the exercise at this stage is taken in the form of walking.

Another doctor, Jack Scaff MD, is so convinced that patients can make a very good recovery that he enters some of them for the Boston Marathon! After careful training of course. Seven middle-aged former heart-attack patients being treated by Dr Kavanaugh made the newspaper headlines in 1973 when they completed the marathon. They were closely monitored throughout the race and they reported no heart or respiratory problems at all.

Naturally most heart-attack patients would not like to be training for a marathon — even before their heart-attack — and for them half an hour of brisk walking every day can work wonders for their recovery.

The feats of the marathon runners, however, do provide a graphic illustration of the point that exercise is the key to a safe recovery. And you cannot have any safer exercise than walking.

Finally, for those who still have doubts, listen to what an American real estate executive had to say. He was 72 years old and 3 years after retiring at the age of 69 he had a massive heart attack which necessitated a double-bypass operation and the fitting of a pacemaker. Three months after these operations he began his cardiac rehabilitation programme which involved walking every day and a three times weekly work-out on an exercise bicycle. All the time that he was exercising his efforts were being carefully monitored by a nurse. After eight weeks of this routine the executive actually returned to normal daily activities. He said: 'I can't say enough about my exercise programme. It makes me feel stronger and healthier.'

Dr Robert Cantu in his book *Toward Fitness* (Human

Sciences Press, 1980) goes even further than this, saying: 'It is my belief that with a professionally supervised exercise programme, many heart attack victims may not just return to work, *but they may restore their hearts to a state far better than before the heart attack.'*

There *is* hope, but you need confidence, patience and clearance from your heart specialist before starting your programme of walking. But walking is the way back to health, without a doubt.

Recovery after Surgery

'Convalescence' is a word seldom heard now. Rarely do those who have been ill spend a recuperative period devoted entirely to bed rest and letting the world drift by until their strength returns. A new and more positive term is used — 'active rehabilitation'. This is a purposeful routine which makes the patient fit in every respect — physically, mentally, and socially — and enables him to lead as full a life as possible.

For those who have undergone surgery, medical rehabilitation begins when the patient fumbles through the thinning clouds of anaesthesia and finds that the angelic presence beside the bed is none other than the hospital physiotherapist waiting to help with the breathing exercises.

For others also, when the crisis of the illness has passed, the rehabilitation road is open, and the hospital staff will be there to give them a helping hand for their first short walk down the corridor.

At first, it might seem to the patient that the emphasis of the activity is mainly on muscular development and also the redevelopment of co-ordination and skill, but there are wider benefits to be gained from light exercise in which walking features predominantly.

A visit from a cheerful physiotherapist can do more than mobilise joints and tone up muscles. It can be a tonic for the whole person. Instead of brooding about their infirmity, patients can be distracted into doing something for themselves, taking steps towards their own recovery. The very act of working for this contributes tremendously to complete rehabilitation.

Furthermore, the physiotherapist who visits regularly often wins the confidence of the patient and learns of any worries or problems. To solve these speeds recovery too. Physiotherapists who start their patients walking back to better health can do much to give the patient confidence and motivation. Walking is the least strenuous of all forms of aerobic exercise and it is especially suited to those who need to build up physical strength and psychological assurance. It is especially good for those patients who were inactive for many years before they fell ill.

What such people appreciate with walking is the way that they can keep track of their progress from week to week. Measurable success motivates them further and soon they learn to enjoy walking and they are therefore likely to continue with it when they have recovered from their illness.

The pleasant exercise of walking has another bonus for those who are ill in hospital or at home; it relieves boredom and makes the muscles pleasantly tired so that sleep comes more easily. And sleep, of course, is a great healer — the sleep that knits up the ravelled sleeve of care, as Macbeth put it.

Walking to a Better Night's Rest

One of the ways John Birt, the Deputy Director of the BBC, copes with the pressure of his life is to leave time for solitude. He says, 'The danger is working so hard you have no time to reflect.' Time for reflection is the recipe which doctors recommend for those recovering from illness — a reflective walk taken last thing at night with a good companion or alone — clears the mind and composes it for a good night's rest.

Karl Miele, the washing machine millionaire of Gütersloh, North-Rhine-Westphalia, told the writer that once following a period of illness his doctors recommended late night walks. 'I found it was just what I needed. Some people can relax with yoga, but I found a long, leisurely, lone walk really destressed me. I've kept it up ever since. I find myself humming tunes of my younger days, almost like a Buddhist monk chanting. I never have any need for sleeping pills.'

The late night walk should not be strenuous for those recovering from illness, but just taxing enough to leave the body joyously fatigued so that it puts the mind in a tranquil mood that ensures a beneficial sleep.

Stiff and Painful Joints

Nobody feels like taking exercise if there is pain and stiffness in the joints. Yet without exercise the condition often worsens: the joints become stiffer still and the muscles surrounding them atrophy with disuse. Fortunately, the problem is not as perverse as it may seem. Relief from stiff and painful joints can now more often be provided than in former days. Pain can be alleviated and some joint mobility restored. Obviously, not every condition can be successfully treated, but prospects are brighter than they used to be.

Many arthritis sufferers have found that walking helps alleviate the symptoms of the disease without putting undue strain on tender joints. However, treatment which is successful with one individual may aggravate the condition in another. Consequently, specialist advice must be sought before subjecting joints and the surrounding tissue to drastic walking routines.

Most treatment routines for arthritis are based on a combination of drugs and exercise. The drugs are to control and reduce pain, while exercise, properly prescribed, maintains a degree of mobility and prevents joints seizing up. But because each individual needs specific treatment it is important that you tell your doctor if a drug or form of exercise causes more pain. Walking and all forms of exercise should be avoided when the joints are swollen or inflamed. Indeed when the condition is in this severe stage the best treatment is often found to be bed rest with aspirin to relieve pain.

If you are able to walk then progress gradually and combine it with swimming. Walking, swimming and specific exercises for the affected joints are good not only for the direct symptoms of arthritis, but also for your general health. There is also an opportunity for active participation with friends which boosts morale.

There cannot be any true anatomical cure for arthritis because of the inability of cartilage to regenerate itself. Nevertheless, walking can do much towards alleviating the symptoms.

One final piece of advice often given to arthritic patients is to lose weight. When painful and damaged joints are being asked to carry an unnecessary load, the rate of joint degeneration is speeded up and the symptoms of pain are aggravated.

12

Walk For Your Life

'A five-mile walk will do more good to an unhappy but healthy adult than all the medicine and psychology in the world.'

Dr Paul Dudley White

The average housewife walks 52 miles between Monday and Friday each week. This was revealed by a new study by shoe manufacturers, Scholl, which was reported in the Daily Express of 14 March 1988. This is two and a half times the distance covered by their office-bound husbands and four times that walked by working mothers.

To put it another way, in a year the housewife walks an average of 3,440 miles — the distance from London to New York. The figures certainly highlight the disparity between the walking exercise taken by different categories of people and surely emphasises the need for the office-bound husband, and the working mother, to do some extra walking exercise. For in most cases walking will probably be the only exercise they do take.

You might be an urban walker of some months or even years, but even so there could still be times when you might weaken enough to wonder whether you will be able to keep it up.

It is a question worth facing squarely, for the alternative could be a dismal tailing-off and ultimate abandonment of your whole urban walking programme and consequent loss of fitness. Self-questioning is natural. What you need to do now is to arm yourself with ways of bolstering your resolution. Here are some useful tips which will help you to avoid falling prey to any number of silly excuses for walking less.

Here, then, is how to stay with your walking programme.

Harness the Driving Force

A great deal of publicity has recently been given to the value of mental power and positive thinking. Walking is important to you for your health, for your future and for your happiness. You are in fact walking for your life. You might already have experienced the benefits walking has brought to you. Now you are going to safeguard those benefits and build upon them. You are going to develop the same will to succeed that turns successful athletes into champions. They call it the will to win.

Everybody wants to win, but few have the ability to pour every ounce of fuel into their game and develop that intense will to win that overcomes all difficulties. Indeed, those who have studied the lives of world-beaters are continually surprised to discover what handicaps they have had to overcome by sheer guts and determination. These champions have a mental power which drives them to greater feats than were thought possible. Often they become champions against the odds.

Similarly, we can frequently see for ourselves, and often read in the daily press, how 10 tired men on a soccer pitch can fight with so much spirit that instead of being severely handicapped by being a player short, they rise above themselves and play better than they did when all 11 were there. This is another forceful demonstration of the power of the mind to drive the body on to extraordinary efforts. They believe that they can win and so, often against the odds, they do.

But this tremendous effect of the mind on the body does not apply only to competitive sports which attract excited spectators. It applies also to your walking. The right attitude of mind is as essential to the success of your urban walking programme as it is to the professional golfer or tennis player. These champions know only too well the importance of this mental power.

Take US Open Golf Champion, Johnny Miller, for example. He invested £6,000 on a week-long course run by psychologist Chuck Hogan of Oregon. As a result Miller regained his lost form. 'You learn how to banish all negative thoughts and tell yourself, "this shot is a piece of cake," and so you hit it well.'

Walkers can profit from this sort of experience. Think positively about why you are walking and all the benefits to be gained. Banish all negative thoughts and doubts. Develop that powerful 'will to win', to succeed in keeping up with your walking programme.

Gaining Support

Just as a football team can be spurred on by a crowd of supporters so too can the urban walker's resolution. Walking with a colleague, or with friends, gives you the spur to be there each morning because you don't want to let anyone down. Walking together gives a feeling of shared achievement. As you walk together and talk together you have the opportunity of testing just how well-adjusted your pace is. Remember you should be walking just fast enough so that you can carry on a conversation without having to gasp for breath.

There will be mornings when, if you are walking alone, you might not feel like walking quite as briskly as you should. But when you walk with someone else, you keep up with the other's pace and so help each other.

Support at home can be crucial. An investigation carried out by the Heart Disease and Stroke Control Programme proved this point. Men taking part in this programme had to complete an hour's strenuous physical activity, three times a week for eight months. Some men attended regularly, some dropped out. The determining factor was the degree of support provided by the wife; if she encouraged the husband he attended well. If she was indifferent or critical the attendance was poor.

You will need all the support you can get. We have already seen the value of group activity with the success of slimming clubs, like Weight-Watchers. Walking with a partner or friends can provide similar support. It helps everyone to keep going.

Set Precise Long-Term Aims

Be sure of exactly what you are aiming to achieve. It's no good saying, 'I'm walking to get fitter', neither would it be of much use to say, 'I'm aiming to lose some weight'. You have to be precise. You need to be able to measure just how much fitter you want to be and how much weight you want to lose and in how much time. These are realistic aims and progress towards them can be measured. Test your physical fitness with the step test routine. (See page 37.) Note how much progress in your heart rate recovery score you make over the months. This will spur you on to further efforts. The key to success is in having the aims clearly written out and the progress towards them recorded.

Set Yourself New and Interesting Goals

Be imaginative. You can bring interest into your walking programme by planning imaginary journeys based upon the distances you manage to walk each week. For example, one man worked out that you could walk up the height of Mount Everest, the world's highest mountain, if you climbed the average house staircase 30 times a day. Work it out for yourself. There are usually 13 steps, each 8 inches high. Multiply this by 30, divide by 12 and you will see that you climb 260 feet in one day. Everest is 29,000 feet high or thereabouts, and so, in 15.9 weeks (to be exact) you could have reached the height of the summit of Everest: without oxygen!

You could imagine walking from Land's End to John O'Groats, or along the Appalachian Scenic Trail which is 2,000 miles long. Have a chart on your bedroom wall with a straight line representing the total distance to be covered. Mark on it all the major towns to be passed. Try to work out an itinerary so that you have to arrive at certain places at given times. This can force you to keep to a previously planned schedule. Have a target date for completing the journey and plan to let yourself have a treat on the day the long walk is completed.

Such imaginary journeys can generate new interests and can help to systematically build up your strength and stamina to acceptable levels, and you will be able to have the satisfaction of seeing progress every day. Don't take the idea so seriously that you begin to compete with yourself too strenuously. Increase the distance walked daily only gradually as your condition improves. How fast you are walking is not important at the outset. It is where you are going that matters.

Pick Yourself Some New Routes

The choice of routes is not altogether unlimited, but there can be variations. There is not a lot to be gained from walking the same route every day just because it is the more direct one. There could be old rights of way to seek out: corridors created from now-abandoned railways, transmission lines, canal tow-paths, paths along river banks, aqueducts, pipelines or abandoned roads.

Try a diversion to explore back-cuts and other streets and make opportunities for extra walking on other occasions. Tony Nicholson is a great believer in getting back to basics, living a full life and using his body as it was meant to be used — actively. He told me:

> When I take my girl-friend out to dinner, we park the car in a quiet suburb and walk the rest of the way hand in hand. It's the same when we take in a show. This I think is the natural way, more romantic. There's a lot you can tell each other without saying a word — just in the way that you hold each other's fingers and palm of the hand. You can't have any of that feeling of discovery driving through traffic, searching for a parking place as close as possible to your destination.

There are some beautiful old residential areas and quaint streets that meander through beautiful old estates which can provide delight as you walk. Take care that you wear reflective strips when you are walking at night. Be on the alert for all sorts of hazards — walk defensively.

Watch out for Sabotage

There will be times when, as you are walking along the road towards your transport stop in the morning, a friendly neighbour will draw up his car alongside the kerb, lean over and open the door for you to hop in, assuming that your car is in the garage for a service. Be firm. Have your answer ready to avoid embarrassment for yourself or your kindly neighbour. Tell him you need the exercise or the fresh air. Some people seem almost to resent other people taking exercise walking; they are critical of what they call 'your fitness walking craze'. Laugh with them, but go your own way.

Betty Wingard, one of the few women oil traders in the city, weighed 14 stone 6 pounds before she abandoned her midday canteen lunches and walked for half an hour instead. She also joined Weight Watchers, who told her exactly what her goal weight should be, and in 12 months she was given her gold pin for reaching the target. 'The walking helped in many ways,' she said, 'It took me away from others who were eating, I could relax with an orange in the park and I came back to work refreshed. I still found that there were some girls in the office who adopted a queer attitude to my walking, though whether it was through envy or perversity in wishing to lead me back into the lunch-time group, I don't know. But I told them I wasn't being unsociable, just desperate to get into a bikini again one day.'

Make Habit Work for You

Needless repetitive decision-making is wasteful of effort. You should not have to decide each day the time when you are going to walk. Keep to a routine that leaves you free and with adequate time for your walk at whichever time of day suits you best. The rest of the day's events can then revolve around those fixed times. Naturally there will have to be some flexibility, but the more that you keep to a regular pattern the easier it will be for you to keep it going.

The main point is to think everything through well ahead. Sometimes you might decide to rethink the whole programme asking yourself, for example, whether it might be more advantageous at certain times of the year to do more of your walking in the suburbs rather than at the city end of your journey. There could be financial advantages in some replanning to make the best of fare stages and stations.

Does the walk after work give you adequate time to unwind so that you arrive home free of the day's accumulation of tension? Consider also whether a late evening walk — with or without your spouse or partner — would give you the enjoyment of breathing fresh air into respiratory tubes clogged by dry centrally heated air. Such late evening walks are relaxing both physically and mentally. 'It's the best sleeping aid ever invented,' wrote Charles Kuntzleman, editor of the Consumer Guide and a dedicated walker.

Read through Your Walking Record at Regular Intervals

Note well, all the good work you have already put in. What a pity it would be if all that should be wasted! For let there be no mistake, if you once stop walking then the training would have been in vain. Fitness gained is quickly lost through inactivity. Some experts say that it takes a month of reconditioning exercise to make up for each year of physical inactivity that has gone before. It is always easier to keep going than to make a fresh start later.

Think back to how you were perhaps shocked to discover just how unfit you were after your first 15-minute session of brisk walking. You would not like to have to be in that state again, would you?

Seek Management Backing

There is no doubt that more people would be tempted to take to the urban walking regime if they could be assured of adequate facilities at their offices for changing clothes and even having a shower. If no such facilities exist, it could be worthwhile putting the case to senior management, pointing out that the outlay could well be recouped in terms of better attendance, fewer cases of sickness and a livelier and happier workforce.

The Ford Motor Company in Dearborn has gone to great lengths to encourage staff to take more exercise. The company has produced a physical activity called the Headquarters Hustle. Dr Beverly Ware, Corporate Health Education Coordinator at Ford, worked out a plan whereby an employee could go down to the Health Services Department and obtain a map of the whole plant showing distances measured between various points. Employees could then work out their own daily walking course. It was a programme that took off and worked well for everyone.

'We wanted the employees to know that they could do something constructive in their working clothes and in a relatively short time right there on the work site, despite not having physical facilities for an exercise programme on location,' explained Dr Ware.

Are you Making the Best Use of 'Overload'?

The principle of 'overload' is fundamental to all strengthening exercise routines. Walking will strengthen your leg muscles, your heart muscle, those of the shoulder girdle and many other muscles. You can use 'overload' to make your walking routine more effective and interesting. The way overload works has been explained in this way in Eric Taylor's *Progressive Weight Training* (Springfield, 1988). If you pick up a pen, only a small proportion of the fibres of the arm flexor muscles work; pick up a crowbar and a very high proportion need to work. If the crowbar is lifted repeatedly, other fibres in the muscles are brought in to give the fatigued fibres time to rest and recover. The load is thus shunted from one set of fibres within the muscle to another. But if an even heavier crowbar is used, a still greater proportion of muscle fibres is needed to perform the same movement and there is less opportunity for tiring fibres to rest. Soon the muscle becomes fatigued and the work stops. If the work were done regularly, the fibres of the muscle involved would develop so that the narrower fibres would become stronger, and fewer of them would need to be stimulated at one time to do the same amount of work as before. The navvy's muscles become bigger with use and he can work for a long time before they become fatigued.

It can be seen, then, that when muscles are exercised against heavier weights they are exercised more thoroughly and each fibre works almost to its capacity before becoming fatigued. The onset of fatigue is eventually delayed by hypertrophy of the muscle. It is a natural and beneficial development. Systematic 'overloading' affects the muscle in more than one way. Not only do the individual fibres increase in size and strength, but the control of the muscle by the central nervous system also improves. With greater strength and better nervous control, the trained muscles show a marked improvement in stamina too.

We are not considering here the development of phenomenal strength, for it may seldom be needed, but it is a fact that strong people can move moderate loads, including their own body weight, more easily and with less fatigue. They are consequently in a fitter state physically at the end of the day to enjoy their leisure. Walkers can apply the principle of overload to their routines to achieve more effective training.

Gary D. Yanker, author of the *Complete Book on Exercise Walking* recommends 'weight-loaded walking'. By adding extra weight to your body you can burn more calories per minute, tax your muscles more severely and get more out of every minute of brisk walking than you would from normal walking. Furthermore you are adding interest to your routine.

Weight can be added either by using a small back pack in which the urban walker can carry spare shoes, books and maybe a little extra weight of some other convenient nature. A back pack is more comfortable than carrying a brief case in one hand as this destroys the balance of the body. You can increase your calorie burning rate by up to one third by adding additional weight to your trunk.

Once again, though, do not become too enthusiastic and overdo the weight-loaded walking. Watch out for warning signs of extra sweating and heavier than normal breathing and do remember that your walking is meant to be fun!

Becoming the 'Ultra Walker'

When the urban walker wishes to break out of the city streets, a network of forests, nature reserves and National Parks beckons with well-marked trails, most of which do not involve too much climbing.

And once the urban walker is bitten by the 'ultra' walking bug then a whole mass of new pleasures suddenly becomes available. Magazines will tell you where to go for bird-watching, rambling, observing wild-life, wine bibbing or whatever else you wish. Ask at the nearest Tourist Information Office for details of walks and theme trails in the neighbourhood. Then, when you have explored all these, you could be ready for the more challenging walks at home and abroad.

These will not only stretch your legs, but your horizons too. You can enjoy planning these trips which could test your stamina for six hours or for six weeks. Most of these walks will be at vacation times and then you can use your urban walking as the preparatory and conditioning physical training for a memorable adventure walk. Thus your daily walk through the city can take on a completely new meaning. These challenge or adventure walks could be self-guided trips or you could join professionally guided parties. And you are never too old to start.

One retired headmistress now spends most of her time preparing for such trips or in recovering from them. In the last three years she has been up Kilimanjaro, into the Andes, across Tibet and into China. 'I'm having a marvellous time and feel 10 years younger', she says. 'Previously the only real outdoor activity I had was in walking through two miles of Manchester suburb to school each morning. I used to be counting the days then to retirement, and felt that my morning walk and the walk home in the evening was all part of the preparation for my retirement. Now the world's my oyster!'

She has also found it a challenge — walks have been an adventure in other ways too — having to share a bivouac tent with men and women she had never met before, for example.

At home in England, organisations such as the Wayfarers' Association specialise in holidays with literary themes. Bryn Patterson went on one of these, and got hooked on Thomas Hardy.

I'd only been bored with Hardy's Mayor of Casterbridge at school when we had to swot it up for examinations, but I was persuaded to go on this walking trip by my girl-friend. The walk started from Dorchester — Hardy's Casterbridge — and we were with a group of other cheerful first timers. Very soon we were steeped in the past where people walked everywhere they wanted to go, even if it took all day, and where very few ever travelled outside of their home district; where hours of work were long, from dawn till dusk; where life was hard without the frantic rush of modern day high technology and high pressure. And before I knew what was happening I was reading the Mayor of Casterbridge again with fresh eyes, finding it to be a story with many twists and surprises. It far exceeded the everyday level of my own experiences. And I learnt some fundamental truths of life. That walk opened up literature to me and literature has opened up a whole new world.

The Wayfarers' Hardy walk took the group through the localities in which the action took place, into an area rich in peaceful villages and pastoral landscapes. Rides were available for those who got too tired or hungry for the Stilton cheese or Cornish pasties waiting for them at the evening's bed and breakfast stop-over.

The Next Step

You too could graduate from urban walking to the challenge walks of Britain, Europe and America. Imagine the excitement, for example, of walking through Tuscany's medieval walled towns and following ancient footpaths towards Romanesque churches. Or, if you wish to whet your appetite for excitement still further, what about the ultimate walks in Nepal where a centuries-old system of footpaths traverses the foothills of the Himalayas of Central Asia? In this area, which boasts eight of the world's ten highest mountains, nine American women, ranging in age from six to seventy, recently made an eight-day trek from Pokhara to Ghandrung in the Annapurna region and back. They walked through busy villages, crossed swaying rope bridges over tumbling mountain streams, climbed through rice paddies into fragrant rhododendron forests and at the end of it they all came back with an unforgettable feeling of exhilaration.

This is living!

And now it's all open to you too. Once you have made your choice, return to your urban walking with renewed enthusiasm. Who knows, this could be what your urban walking has really been all about!

13
Calculated Risk

In some people there is an impulse that makes them want to climb mountains, hurtle down a 90-foot ski jump, or to drive a car faster than any man on earth. It is a spirit of adventure. There is an equally potent driving force which appears as ambition in others who want to reach the top in a profession, business or creative art.

Neither of these forces can be quenched by advice to take it easy. But to the mountaineer, ski-jumper and racing motorist the dangers are evident, risks can be calculated, and physical preparation is part of the planning for success. The ambitious must plan too. Though the risks for them are not as exciting nor as evident they are just as real, and ignoring them does not remove them.

Most of us are ambitious. We fix our sights on a target and set out to overcome all difficulties by energetic effort, but there is a limit to the strain a body can stand. We need to keep it fit. With this most people would agree: few really dispute the value of regular exercise, of keeping body weight within bounds, and of balancing work with play, but because time is so short 'tomorrow will do' is often the attitude adopted.

Tomorrow may be too late.

When it comes to keeping fit we are inclined to gamble, to put off for a few days, weeks or years the action we should take now. Sometimes it is a justifiable and calculated risk but more often it is likely to be mere procrastination, foolhardy and irresponsible. We allow ourselves to be pushed on by the pressure of events and the driving force within. We say we are too busy and have no time for relaxation and physical recreation. It is a short-sighted policy which inevitably takes its toll.

Well then, what is the answer? It is so easy to give advice and to run other people's lives and yet so difficult to order our own. Nevertheless, difficult though it may be, if we accept the fact that fitness should be maintained, we must then pause to consider the best practical means of achieving that end. Somehow the week has to be planned with the same thoroughness as the mountaineer plans his expeditions so that the known risks can be tackled with the maximum expectancy of success.

We all know the risks of sedentary living; they have been publicised enough. Now we have to decide how we are going to minimise those risks so that we can enjoy a longer, healthier, more productive and satisfying life.

At this point in the book there should be little doubt in the mind of the reader that we must now aim to modify our behaviour and our life-style. We must turn that sedentary individual into a person who pleasurably and regularly takes part in an exercise programme. A person who pays no heed whatsoever to that dangerous little voice that pipes up within saying: 'Pack it up. It's not worth the effort.'

Once you have started your urban walking programme things become much easier, your cardio-vascular system increases in capacity, your muscles get stronger, your body becomes more flexible and you will be experiencing that 'high' sensation that brings a feeling of euphoria after exercise. The physical and mental benefits will provide all the incentive you need to continue your walking programme.

To recapitulate, at the risk of being repetitious, walking is the recommended exercise for people of all ages and all physical conditions. It is safe and efficacious, it presents no problem for the older walker with more vulnerable hips, ankles and lower body joints. It is recommended for those who are overweight because it is the least strenuous of all aerobic exercise. It is even recommended for those who have arthritis. Indeed, as we have already seen, some sufferers find that walking helps the symptoms of the disease and improves muscular flexibility. Some emphysema patients have been helped by walking routines and of course, walking is *de rigueur* for recuperation of heart patients. In short, walking is so easy to start and to work into the daily urban routine that it is the ideal activity for everyone who wishes to improve their physical fitness.

And what is more, it can lead to all kinds of exciting developments. You will find yourself looking forward to it, almost longing for it as an accustomed pleasure.

Index